CONTENTS

Copyright

Free Market Capitalism and The U.S. Constitution   2

Part I   4

   Chapter 1 The Humans   6

   Chapter 2 Emergence of Money   8

   Chapter 3 Why Sound Money   16

   Chapter 4 Why a Free Market   28

   Chapter 5 Government's role in the Free Market   40

   Chapter 6 What Laws Should We Have?   46

   Chapter 7 Decentralized Governence   54

   Chapter 8 Funding The Government   68

   Chapter 9 The Pinnacle   76

Part II   86

   Chapter 10 Dealing with Corporations   90

   Chapter 11 Indecent Goods and Services   124

   Chapter 12 Spending For The Common Good   138

   Chapter 13 Financial Crises & Boom-Bust cycle   176

   Chapter 14 Concluding Remarks   190

References   194

Contact   198

FREE MARKET CAPITALISM AND THE U.S. CONSTITUTION

THE ANTIDOTE TO AUTHORITARIANISM

PART I

Establishing The Ideal Society By Building From The Ground Up

CHAPTER 1

The Humans

From a reductive point of view, humans are just a species that was the best at surviving amongst many other species. To an extraterrestrial observer, there would be The Humans, The Lions, The Zebras, etc. Looking at humans on this grand scale, we can observe that we are each an individual human, but we are also a part of the human race. We are Team Human! All lifeforms on Earth overcome daily challenges with the ultimate goal of making more copies of themselves. What is it that makes The Humans better at overcoming obstacles than other species? Why did we rise to the top?

The answer is the ability to form societies with other members of our species. In fact, humans are so social that the worst thing you can do to a prisoner is to put them in a room by themselves. The pain of separating from other humans is deeply rooted in our evolutionary brains.

Our deep-driven quest for socialization allows us, humans, to form societies. Rather than each individual taking care of themselves, we can focus on specific tasks and collectively produce more. While your neighbor catches fish, you take care of the farm, and someone else builds houses. *We can collectively produce more like this* because at any given job, say fishing, the cost of catching one extra fish for a Fisherman is less than the cost for a newcomer catching his first fish. This is not just due to the skills required. If a Fisherman is to provide for ten people, he can **invest** in a net, which decreases the cost of acquiring extra fish.

Compare this to a case where ten individuals would each catch their own fish. Knowing that the Fisherman will provide food for you, you can devote your energy to your task at hand, which is, let's say, farming. Since you now must farm for more people than just yourself, you invest in tools that make you more **efficient** at farming.

In this example, the Fisherman and the Farmer are **entrepreneurs,** which is essentially a fancy word for someone who solves problems for a given need. Notice that society overall was able to **output** more, and therefore the individuals could enjoy more **goods and services**. Using economic terms, one would say that the Gross Domestic Product, the **GDP,** of this society has increased. GDP measures the *gross,* meaning total amount, of *product,* meaning goods and services, produced *domestically,* meaning specifically in some defined region. It is, therefore, just a measure of a society's output. The increase in output comes from the **division of labor**, where each individual focuses on what they make best, and **investment,** where tools like fishnets are used in production. Another name for tools is **capital.** Specialization leads to investments in capital, which makes workers more efficient and consequently increases the total goods and services produced, also called the GDP.

Now you understand why the world focuses on GDP so much. It's a measure of how much "stuff" we created. Those who make moral arguments criticizing society's emphasis on GDP, but a lack of focus on helping each other, have a faulty understanding of economics. *GDP is a measure of how much we have helped each other.* It is precisely that. Everything is produced because someone somewhere needs it. By increasing the GDP, we end up satisfying more needs of the people.

Notice that this efficient society depends on one critical piece: the ability of our Farmer and Fisherman to **trade.** If they can't trade, they will both eat what they can, and the rest will rot. In other words, all the extra efficiency that came from tools and division of labor will be wasted. This is why it's critical that there be a **market** where goods and services can be exchanged freely. Civilizations from all over the world have all had markets where citizens can exchange goods and services with one another. This is the fundamental difference between The Humans and other species.

We survive better because we have more goods and services to help us overcome the challenges nature poses. *We have more goods and services because we can freely trade in markets.*

CHAPTER 2

Emergence of Money

From Barter To Gold

How does money come into play? What even is money? Before money, we had **bartering**, which is a system of direct exchange of two goods or services with one another. Bartering is problematic because if you sell potatoes and you need a chair, you need to find someone who sells chairs and needs potatoes. This brings about a need for a **medium of exchange**. A medium of exchange is an intermediary commodity that the market participants can trade in and out of. They first acquire the medium of exchange by trading what they produced for it and later acquire what they want by trading the medium of exchange with a producer of the good or service they desire.

Theoretically, it could be anything, and for the sake of example, let's say the medium of exchange for some hypothetical civilization is cows. Everything is priced in units of cows, so you sell your potatoes for some cows, and then you can use your cows to buy chairs or anything for that matter. Trading just got way more manageable, but individuals are not so happy. To start off, not all cows are the same. Cows aren't divisible, so nothing can be bought for less than "1-cow." It is challenging to store cows (which are your savings). Walking them to the market is a hassle. They need to be fed, and sometimes they die. This makes the society at hand think that cows are not such suitable mediums of exchange.

They decide that they need something: **divisible**, so smaller units of account can be made; **durable**, meaning it doesn't die, decay, deteriorate, etc.; **portable**, meaning carrying it to the market is easy;

and **recognizable**, meaning one does not need to inspect it much to know that it's real. They decide on gold because it happens to be a metal that satisfies all these properties. It is a metal that is easily broken into smaller pieces, it doesn't rust, it's easy to carry, and it can be tested to verify legitimacy. But that is not the only reason they decide to use gold.

The final desirable quality of money is **consistent scarcity,** meaning the quantity does not change or it changes slowly. Consistent scarcity allows the medium of exchange to preserve its value. In other words, it ensures that one's savings today will be worth the same tomorrow. This fact follows a simple logic. The fewer there is of something, the more valuable it will be. There is a link between value and scarcity. Therefore, if the scarcity of something is nearly constant, its value is nearly constant.

For example, if you owned the only banana in the world, people would exchange very valuable things for it. But if it started raining bananas the next day, so much that the streets flooded with bananas, you would find that your banana had lost most of its value. In other words, people would trade you less precious items for your banana. Or for example, spices, and even salt, used to be extremely valuable. Now, with the advancement of technology, there is so much salt that it is practically free. If you sold everything you had for some salt back in the day and waited until now, you would have a net worth near zero. Alternatively, if you sold everything you had for some gold, you would be pretty rich because the supply of gold has only minimally increased.

Careful readers may have noticed a possible contradiction. We said that an investment in gold back in the days would have made you rich now because its supply only increased minimally. However, we had also said that the more there is of something, the less it is worth. So, how come gold is more valuable if its supply, though marginally, has still increased? If anything, gold should be slightly less valuable. Indeed, it is true that every increase in the gold supply makes the existing gold less valuable, but the key is to notice that the supply of everything else is also increasing. As society becomes more productive, it can produce more of all goods and services. That means that all goods and services become less valuable. However, since gold's supply increases much slower than the supply of almost everything else, it loses the least value.

A nice analogy would be to visualize all goods and services as elevators. The first elevator represents gold. The second represents bananas, the third represents salt, and so on with all goods and services. The height of an elevator represents its value. Over time, we produce more of everything, so all elevators go down. But the gold elevator goes down very slowly. To the people in most elevators, the gold elevator appears to be moving upwards when in fact, all elevators are moving down.

Gold, as you can see, satisfies all the desired properties of money, and for that reason, it has been a medium of exchange for thousands of years. Notice how it has naturally emerged as a medium of exchange because it excelled at the necessary properties of being money and not by the decree of some government.

We call mediums of exchange that satisfy the aforementioned desired properties: **sound money**.

To Paper Backed By Gold

Up until 1971, the world was still using gold for money. Even though it was through roundabout ways, money was effectively backed by gold. The effects of removing the backing have been devastating both economically and socially. Most people don't even know the price of gold today, but gold used to be the center of attention in the world. So how did people go from shiny precious metals to paper? It didn't happen all at once. The story begins with the transition from using physical metal gold to paper backed by gold.

Briefly, as civilizations used gold to trade, several problems emerged. People tried cheating the system by using metals visually similar to gold or by making alloys of gold and thus devaluing the coin. The solution was to have a trustable entity that would mint coins with a unique stamp. The entity makes sure the metal is indeed gold and that it is pure.

However, other problems emerged. People were clipping pieces off the edges of each coin and making new coins from these clippings. Ridges were added to the perimeters of coins to make any clipping obvious. Even modern coins have ridges on the perimeter even though there are no precious metals in the coins.

The final issue was the denomination of the coins. Buyers and sellers wanted to price their goods and services precisely, but making coins smaller than a particular denomination was difficult. Imagine going to the store today and instead of seeing prices listed as (1.01, 1.02, 1.03); you saw: ($1\frac{1}{8}, 1\frac{2}{8}, 1\frac{3}{8}$.) All these problems could be easily avoided by creating a trusted entity to hold all the gold, which would then issue receipts for the gold deposits. You give this entity 1 ounce of gold and receive a piece of paper that entitles you to an ounce of gold. You can now trade these receipts conveniently and even go to the entity to demand one hundred "0.01-ounce papers" instead of one "1-ounce paper."

Technically, anyone can solve the aforementioned problems. They would need to verify that the given metal is indeed gold, mint it into a coin with a verifiable sign, add ridges to the side, and keep it in safe storage until the owner redeems it using his gold deposit receipt. This would make them a **bank**. Here is a privately issued note from such a bank from 1853.

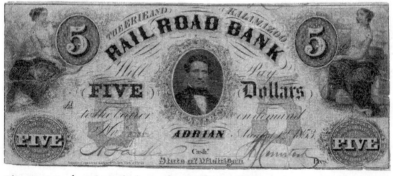

Figure 2.1: A privately issued note from 1853

There is also a central bank of the United States called the Federal Reserve, or FED. The receipts issued by this bank are called Federal Reserve Notes. Below is a picture of a Federal Reserve Note.

Figure 2.2: Federal Reserve Note from 1914.

The image belongs to the National Numismatic Collection at the Smithsonian Institution.

Receipts from all banks function the same way. As it is written on the Federal Reserve Note: "Redeemable in gold on demand at the United States Treasury, or in gold or lawful money at any Federal Reserve Bank." Which, in 1933, meant that $20.67 would entitle you to 1 ounce of gold.

To Paper Backed By Less Gold

The emergence of centralized power in the United States can perhaps best be seen in 1933, when the government made it *illegal to own gold* and demanded that everyone sell their gold to the government. With Executive Order 6102, the government collected all the gold from its citizens at $20.67 per ounce, and immediately following the surrender period, the Gold Reserve Act of 1934 raised the price to $35 per ounce. Every ounce of gold a citizen had saved by working turned into 20/35ths of an ounce of gold. With the stroke of a pencil, the government stole 43% of everyone's savings. It is difficult not to call that authoritarian.

To Paper Backed By A Threat Of Violence

The dollar was ultimately devalued to zero ounces of gold in 1971 when President Nixon publicly broadcasted that he was "temporarily" pausing the convertibility of dollars to gold. Just like that, **fiat money** was born. The word "fiat" is Latin, meaning "let it be done." So you may ask: "How can a piece of paper that is backed by nothing be money?" To which the government would reply: "Because we declared it to be. Let it be money, we said, and it shall be money."

But it cannot be that easy, right? Why does anyone work then? Why can't we also declare that a piece of paper has value? Any time we need to buy something, why can't we just offer a fancy piece of paper with pictures on it that we created? Why do people choose to accept the government's paper but not the one that we create?

The reason U.S. Dollars have value is that you have to pay your taxes in U.S. Dollars. The government can give you paper that is backed by nothing in exchange for something of value because every year, you will need to bring some back in the form of taxes. Even if you go completely off the grid and live in a remote community, even if it is outside of the United States, and even if you trade with gold for the work that you do in this community, you will need to pay taxes to the government. For example, even if you weave baskets in Germany and sell them for gold coins, you will need to calculate your profit by considering the U.S. Dollar value of your gold and pay taxes. This again means that you will need to get your hands on these precious U.S. Dollars.

And what if you don't? Let's say you didn't acquire the dollars to pay your taxes. Then you must try hard to find some as soon as possible because if you are late in paying your taxes, you will owe more taxes. But what if you do not pay those taxes either. Well, then it gets interesting. What happens when you do not abide by any law? Maybe at first, you get larger and larger monetary consequences. But then, when you do not pay those, you get called to court. The court punishes you either in some monetary form, in which case you do not pay and repeat the previous steps, or sends you to jail, which you do not comply with again. You also have the option of not showing up to court, of course, in which case you end up in a similar position, which is when the government wants you to be somewhere, and you do not want to be there. So what happens then? People with guns come to your house and take you. Physically take you. At this point, they have put their hands on you. Keep resisting, and the hands will get tighter. Tasers will come out, guns will be drawn, and more and more force will be applied until you comply. This is the nature of every law. Every single law in the book is backed by a threat of violence. This includes the laws that require you to pay taxes, which the value of the U.S. Dollar depends on. So if the U.S. Dollar has value because you have to pay your taxes with it, and you have to pay your taxes because it is the law, and laws must be abided by because the consequences are violence, then we may conclude that the U.S. Dollar is backed by a threat of violence.

CHAPTER 3

Why Sound Money

A Society With Sound Money

We walked through the history of humanity because we wanted to understand something: Why do The Zebras still look for food all day, living in a constant state of fear due to predation, while The Humans have plenty of food and are making plans to go to different planets? We saw that what differentiated us was our ability to form societies and collaborate. Instead of all 100 of us focusing on our individual survival, we divide up the work and specialize in what we are each good at. This way, each person produces a great amount of whatever good or service he specializes in. He is able to do this because, one, he is better at it than other people, two, it is easier to produce things in bulk, and three, he invests in tools that make him even more productive. Once we each have an abundance of whatever we create, we trade in an open market. After the trading, we each have more than what we would have had if we had individually tried to produce everything. Now, because we have more things, and exactly because of that reason, we are able to survive better. More things enable us to better equip ourselves against the unknowns of nature.

We did run into some problems while trading in the market. We realized that bartering is hard because one must find another person who is looking for exactly what they are selling. Instead, we decided to pick a medium of exchange that we all could trade into and out of. Naturally, this became gold due to its physical properties. There were still some problems: counterfeit gold, the difficulty of small denominations, clipping tiny bits from coins, etc. The solution was an easy one. Keep all the gold somewhere, called a bank, and just trade using the paper certificates that guarantee that the gold is in the bank. It is important to stop here because what then happens to money changes the system entirely. At this point, society is still using sound money, that is, money with intrinsic value and fixed or slow-rising supply. Before exploring society under the fiat money standard, let us gain intuition about the society under sound money.

When an individual earns money in a society with sound money, he does so because he provided something of value to some other person. He **supplied** something that someone **demanded** and received money for doing this. In a basic sense, he **(producer)** sold happiness **(good or service)** to someone **(consumer)** and received a receipt **(money)** indicating the degree to which he made someone happy. So now, the money that he has—entitles him to some happiness when he wants. He can use his money to demand a good or service—and it will be provided to him by someone. It is a fair system because other people make you happy by providing you a good or service, if and only if you have also made someone happy by providing them a good or service. Sound money ensures that the happiness that you provide is exactly equal to the happiness that you receive.

You can imagine the following. As individuals in a society, we each produce goods or services and put these in a metaphorical pot and receive tickets to then claim from this pot. Those tickets are called money. Everyone produces something someone else will consume, and everything you consume is produced by someone else. However, we don't know who exactly produces what and who exactly consumes what, and we do not care. We do not need to keep track of this directly. We only need to make sure that no one takes out from the pot more than they have put into the pot. We use money to ensure this. Precisely, money ensures that no one consumes more than they produce. That is what makes this system fair.

Inequality Rises When The Balance Breaks

Every society needs a way to answer three questions. **What should we produce? How should we produce it? For whom should we produce it?** The process described above answers the "For whom should we produce it?" question. In other words, the "Who gets to take from the pot?" question. We produce things only for people who have also produced things. One can only take from the pot as much as he has put into the pot. But why? Because otherwise, one by one, we would run out of things in the pot. Remember, we survive better as The Humans because we found a way to produce very efficiently and fill our metaphorical pot. If the pot is empty, we are no different than the other animals. Ill-equipped against the dangers of the world. Barely surviving.

This exactly is what happens in communism. Karl Marx himself defines the system as: "From each according to his ability, to each according to his needs." This translates to: "Take from the pot as much as you need and put into the pot as much as you can." A very utopian idea. In order for the things inside the pot to not decrease, as soon as one person takes more than they put in, another person must put in more than they take. But that never happens, so the pot shrinks. Poverty is rampant, and people die from starvation. Society is unhappy and prone to giving one person a lot of power to fix the system. Now this person decides for whom the society must produce. Unsurprisingly, it is his party and his close allies.

There are two types of equilibria in nature. One is a stable equilibrium. An example is a ball in a valley. When the ball is pushed to the right, it experiences a force that rolls it back to the middle. If it is pushed to the left, it experiences a force that rolls it back to the middle. The other type of equilibrium is an unstable equilibrium. It is like a ball on the top of a hill. Theoretically, the ball can remain on the top of the hill forever. If it is exactly in the middle of the hill, it is balanced. However, the equilibrium is unstable because any small deviation to the right or left will accelerate the balls rolling in the same direction. Just a tiny bit of rolling to either the left or right is enough for the ball to roll down the hill. Nevertheless, theoretically, the ball can remain in equilibrium, on top of the hill, indefinitely. Theoretically. Just like how theoretically, you could build an upside-down pyramid. Same logic. Communism is like building an upside-down pyramid. You've done the calculations on paper. All the forces on the left exactly equal the forces on the right. Theoretically, all the excess takers from the pot will equal the excess givers to the pot. But people start cheating. The pyramid starts tilting in one direction. As people get away with cheating, more people cheat. The pyramid's fall accelerates. Eventually, the pyramid collapses, and millions die. But this doesn't stop the upside-down pyramid proponents from claiming that it would not have collapsed if it had been properly tried.

We know, but it is not a perfect world. An upside-down pyramid never works, and we go back to the basics.

What went wrong? We did not maintain a balance between what goes into the pot and what comes out of the pot. We now know that it is essential that we do that. Let's get back on our feet. Our pot is empty, and we need to fill it as fast as possible. How do we begin? Well, there are some resources around us. We can use those. However, they are limited; therefore, we need to make choices. We need to be efficient with our resources because they are limited. Everyone should specialize in one thing, whatever they are good at, and start producing that. Also, we should invest in tools that make us better at producing that thing. This way, we can make the most out of our limited resources. Once you make some things, trade them at the market for other things. What kind of market? Can anyone just show up there? Yes, anyone can come to the market and sell what they want. It is a free market. It is a free market where we sell tools and the things we make using tools. What is another name for tools? Capital. This system is called Free Market Capitalism.

You may be surprised that this nice system where we trade freely and maintain a balance between the inflows and the outflows from the pot is called Free Market Capitalism. But Free Market Capitalism is supposed to be bad. Capitalism is why poor people suffer, right? And Free Market Capitalism? That is the worst form of them all. It is true that the current system in the world mistreats poor people. However, that system is not Free Market Capitalism because our money is not sound. The world currently uses fiat money.

The reason behind the inequality we experience in society right now is the same reason communism led to massive inequality. The communist society broke the market's ability to enforce the requirement that everyone must produce as much as they consume. Instead, it utilized a centralized planner to answer the "for whom to produce" question. When it is not the market that decides how products are rationed but instead a centralized planner, it is not surprising that the centralized planner allocates the products to himself and his allies. This is what leads to unfair inequality. The same thing, to a milder extent, goes on in our society, and fiat money is the biggest enabler of it. In the next section, we will see exactly how fiat money allows a certain class to steal from the poor.

Fiat Money Breaks The Balance

The supply of fiat money can easily change because it is not backed by anything. Printing dollars costs almost nothing. Compare this to a sound money system where the money is backed by gold. In order to increase the supply, one must go to great lengths and mine the little amount of gold left on Earth. Even then, the increase in the supply of gold is beneficial because now society has more of a particular resource. Technically, we would prefer to use gold for every wire we use, but it is too scarce, so we must use other metals. Contrary to paper money, which has no uses, gold has actual uses, so increasing its supply would nevertheless be beneficial. However, this is not the reason why fiat money is detrimental. This is just an explanation of how the money supply can increase easily with fiat money but not with sound money.

But why is it bad if the supply of money changes? In order to see that, we need to understand how the money supply works first. Let's first think of a simple society with 10 people, each with $1, and the metaphorical pot consists of 10 fish. Each fish sells for $1 so each person can eat one fish. The money supply is $10 because there are ten people with $1 each. One of them says: "Vote for me, and I will give everyone $99." Everyone is so excited. They cannot wait to consume 100 fish once they have a total of $100. The person is elected and delivers his promise. All 10 people on the island now have $100 each. They eagerly go to the market to buy fish. One of them, to celebrate his newfound wealth, decides to buy all 10 fish at the market, thinking it would leave him with $90. Little does he know that everyone else also had the same plan. They start a bidding war for the fish and soon realize that the price of one fish has risen up to $100. They eventually each go home with one fish each. The example we just went through increased the money supply by 100 fold. Each person was a hundred times richer than before, but they still went home with one fish. What just happened is **inflation.** They each got richer, but their **purchasing power,** how much product they could buy, did not increase because prices went up by the same amount.

The country of Turkey actually did this in real life, but in reverse. Their money had such a high denomination that everyone was a millionaire. How much is one loaf of bread? 1 million Liras. A pack of gum? 5 million Liras. They decided overnight to drop six zeros from their currency, thereby making every billionaire a thousandaire. However, just as expected, nothing extraordinary happened. The next day, everything went as usual. All the prices were a million times lower. No one was any poorer. This illustrates that money supply changes cannot make a society richer or poorer. The only thing that increases our wealth is what is inside the pot. *If we want to improve society's living conditions, we need to focus on one task only: growing the pot.*

So a money supply change of this sort does not change anything. When everyone receives extra money at the same time, everyone still has the same purchasing power. However, this is not usually how it happens. Consider a second case now. Let us say we want to do the opposite of Turkey and make everyone a millionaire. We will wake up one day, grab a pen, and add six zeros to every dollar bill we have. However, we will do this in two stages. On day 1, 50% of the citizens will add six zeros, and on day 2, the remaining 50%. Now, what will happen? On the first day, the new millionaires have the privilege of shopping for goods and services before the other half. They flood the system with their new money and bid up the price of everything. When it's the turn of the second half, they don't get to enjoy the same luxury as the first half because the price of everything was already bid up. We again changed the supply of money, but it mattered who shopped first. Society, in aggregate, did not get any wealthier because we still have the same amount of things in the pot. However, some people got relatively wealthier compared to others. Specifically the first receivers of the new money. What this means is that society still has the same amount of goods and services, but the distribution of these goods and services has changed. *The early money receivers increased their share of the pot at the expense of the late receivers.*

This is unfair. When one approaches the pot with $1 million, society is under the impression that this person has contributed $1 million worth of goods and services to the pot at some point and, therefore, is now entitled to take out of the pot. However, this is not true since this person has just added six zeros to his $1 dollar. This person has only put $1 worth of goods and services into the pot but has just pulled out $1 million worth of goods and services. The input-output balance of the pot is broken. Therefore, highlighted here is the injustice of the fiat money system.

* * *

We have so far established that money supply changes do not make society richer in aggregate, but it does make the early money receivers relatively richer than the late money receivers. Now let us see who indeed are these early receivers. How does "money printing" work? The institution that is in charge of the money supply is the Federal Reserve. When the FED wants to increase the money supply, it does so by lowering the interest rate at which banks can borrow from Federal Reserve Banks. There is always enough money to be borrowed from the FED because the FED creates the money. When a bank wishes to borrow money from the FED, it will never be rejected. Compare this to yourself. If you say, for example, that someone could borrow money from you at an interest rate of zero, you would soon realize that everyone is knocking on your door. Since you will run out of money like this, you increase your interest rate, discouraging some people from borrowing from you. The FED has no such concern. They can lend forever. The topic of interest rates will be explored later, so for the time being, we should just know that the FED lends to banks at an interest rate to increase the money supply.

The FED also increases the money supply by purchasing bonds from the U.S. Government. Bonds are just promises of payment at a later time. Essentially, by purchasing bonds from the government, the FED is loaning money to the government. This is called Quantitative Easing. It should be clarified that the government cannot tell the FED to purchase its bonds—since they are supposedly independent entities. Their independence is arguable since the President of the United States appoints the chair of the Federal Reserve and since there seems to be a revolving door between the government and various other institutions, exemplified by Janet Yellen, who is the United States secretary of the treasury now, 2021, but was the chair of the Federal reserve from 2014 to 2018. Regardless of whether the FED maintains its independence, the fact of the matter is that the FED makes it easier for the government to borrow money.

The freshly printed dollars, which are not even physically printed but instead digitally brought into existence, make their way to the financial institutions and the government first. Banks loan these dollars to businesses, which technically include small businesses as well, but they also get to use the money themselves. The money does make it to the small businesses, but financial institutions get first dibs. What about the money loaned to the government? That will be spent on certain projects. When deciding on projects, it doesn't forget what those lobbyists were suggesting or what their campaign donors might have wanted. A spending bill is passed, and contracts are awarded to businesses. To be clear, the government does not get to give money to a certain company just because it wants to. There is an open bidding website where contracts are offered to all businesses, and even small businesses are encouraged to partake. However, for example, the backpack industry might lobby the government to pass a "Backpack for Each Kid" bill. Although one company cannot guarantee that it will get the contract, the industry will benefit in general. Or perhaps the government would need the money to bail out a failing industry, like the auto industry.

But even better is a bailout of the financial industry. In the 2008 financial crisis, banks knowingly sold their "bad bets" to their working-class customers, then insured themselves against these bets and left their customers holding the bag. Just to emphasize that again, let's rephrase it. Banks and Rating Agencies at one point realized that the financial products they held were worthless but did not devalue them until they offloaded them to their own customers, for whom they have a fiduciary responsibility to protect, and only devalued them after the offloading was performed and insurance against them was purchased. The government bailed them out regardless.

We went down this path to see who receives the fresh money first and who receives it last. What we see is that the financial industry and the companies that lobby or make campaign donations to the government are the beneficiaries. These are definitely not the working-class people. The poorer part of society receives the money last. Therefore every time new money is spent, the politically connected elite take a little more from the pot than they put in, and the poor end up with a little less from the pot than they contributed. Then our current society is not that different from the top-down communist economies. Our government decides who receives the new money first, and therefore just like the party members in communist counties, they get to decide how to allocate the contents of the pot. They decide who gets to take more than they put in. They get to decide who to enrich and who to impoverish. Over time, we end up with an inequality graph that looks like this.

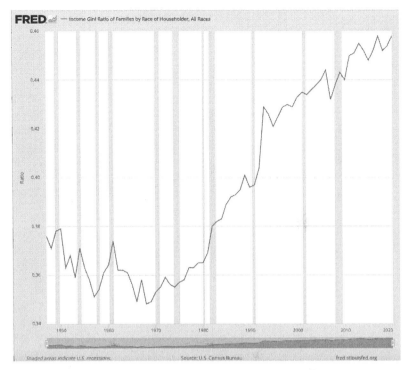

Figure 3.1: Income Gini ratio of families.

The Gini Ratio is a measure of inequality. 0 means everyone has the same income, and 1 means that one person has the highest income while everyone else has no income at all[1]

As you can see, inequality drastically increased after we left sound money in 1971. Fiat money is why the current system is not fair.

When we were walking through the sound money society where everyone specialized in a task and provided to the pot as much as they took, you likely thought it made sense. We started from basic principles and showed that such a society would indeed be fair and prosperous. But likely, you were shocked to hear that it was called Free Market Capitalism. You were always told that the free market is evil. But by whom? Is it the politicians who say this? Aren't those the very people that this system benefits.

The free market is not evil. The free market is fair. The current system is evil and unfair, and it is like that precisely because politicians have too much power. Their power comes from their ability to spend before everyone else, which is thanks to the fiat money system. They tell you that the government needs to spend more and be even more powerful. But, you see, it is exactly that which leads to greater inequality. The politicians who supposedly say they care about the poor are just lying to grab more power. Isn't it at least interesting that Nancy Pelosi's wealth went from $41 million to $115 million from 2004 to 2018, even though her salary is $223,500?[2] Isn't it interesting that Hillary Clinton's "speaker fee" is $225,000, and she requires a private jet, preferably a Gulfstream 450 or larger, a presidential suite with up to three separate rooms attached, and more, and she was booked 92 times between 2013 and 2015?[3] How can they say with a straight face that they represent the shrinking middle class or that they care about inequality?

The intention here is not to only condemn Democrats. Republicans do their fair share of spending exorbitant amounts when they hold power, even though they claim to be "fiscally conservative." And the money printing that Republicans do while they are in office is no less hurtful to the poor than when Democrats do it.

This book should not be politicized like everything in our current society. There is actually a huge uniting factor that both sides of the polarized society must begin to focus on. We are not Republicans who hate the Democrats, nor Democrats who hate Republicans. We are those who are not politically connected—just regular people. We vote for the lesser of the two evils when the time comes. At least A is better than B, we say. We are a part of the silent majority that feels unrepresented in this system but also feels hopeless. But actually, there is hope. We can do one thing. We can realize that the divide is not between the Democrats and the Republicans. It is between the politically connected elite and the common people. Our inability to unite only perpetuates this unfair system. As non-elite people, we have more in common with each other than those who rule over us. We are the last receivers of the newly printed money.

"The forest was shrinking,

but the trees kept voting for the Axe,

for the Axe was clever and convinced the Trees

that because his handle was made of wood,

he was one of them."

- UNKNOWN

CHAPTER 4

Why a Free Market

Voluntary Exchange

Remember the three questions society must answer. What should we produce? How should we produce it? For whom should we produce it? In the last chapter, we explored the "For whom should we produce it?" question. Our answer to this question was that we should produce for only those people who have also put something into the pot. We saw how communism fails because it breaks the equality between what goes into the pot and what comes out, ultimately leading to poverty due to the shrinkage of the pot. Similarly, we saw how fiat money is broken because it enables the early money receivers to take out more than they have put into the pot, ultimately leading to very high inequality. By exploring the "for whom" question, we established that, one, inflows and outflows from the pot must be balanced to ensure that the pot does not shrink, and two, that money should be sound to ensure that we have a fair system. Fair in the sense that no one takes more than they give.

In addition to these, what else do we want in our society? Happiness. As humans, we are cursed with a spell of always wanting more happiness. Whenever we achieve some form of happiness, the feeling of it decays over time, and we must find another thing that makes us happy again. You see this happen very clearly with food. Your initial craving for chocolate makes you seek one. You experience peak happiness when you first taste the chocolate. Then the happiness slowly fades. Soon, you find yourself looking for new forms of happiness.

This is true for even little actions that we typically do not think of as happiness-seeking actions, such as deciding to sit down on a chair. Whilst standing up, why did you suddenly decide to sit down? It is because sitting down would give you more happiness than standing up. Without even bringing it up to your conscious self, your brain quickly calculated that sitting down would give you more happiness than continuing to remain standing up. You know this to be the case because, if given a free choice between two options, you will choose the one that makes you happier. If standing up made you happier than sitting down, you *would* remain standing up. You would never do something that makes you less happy. Eventually, the happiness of another possible action becomes higher than the happiness of sitting down because the happiness of sitting down decays over time. At that exact point, you perform the new activity.

You might be thinking of plenty of examples where you did something that you did not want to do. At some point in your life, you definitely did something that did not make you happy, right? But, most certainly, you forget about a missing variable. If standing up makes you happier than sitting down, but someone puts a gun to your head and tells you to sit down, you will sit down. It is true that standing up gives you more happiness than sitting down; however, the choice here is not between [standing up] and [sitting down]. The trade that your brain contemplates is: "Is the happiness of [standing up + death] higher than that of [sitting down]?" Or, for example, although you are very tired, you choose to go to your friend's dinner party. Although the happiness of [sleeping] is greater than that of the [dinner party], the missing variable is [breaking my friend's heart]. The happiness of [sleeping + breaking my friend's heart] is less than that of [dinner party]; therefore, you go to the party. Humans are always acting in this manner to maximize their happiness with every choice they make as they carve their path through life.

Now, suppose you lived in a society in which sitting down was illegal. You would be less happy as a result of this, right? Your brain wants to trade [standing up] with [sitting down] precisely because it would make you happier to do so. However, since sitting down is illegal, you are unable to perform the trade and are consequently less happy than you could be. What we can see from this example is that people's ability to enact choices should not be limited in a society that wishes to maximize happiness. If a human makes a choice, he does so because he is happier after the choice than before. One exception to this rule must be that the person's choice must only affect himself. For example, he cannot sit down on a delicate sculpture that someone else is working on. We can state our general principle as follows: **people should be free to choose what they want to do, given that they are the only ones affected by their choice.**

These happiness choices that we make, in one way or a form, come from goods and services. Your friend would not have much of a dinner party if there were no dinner, or no chairs, speaker, music, electricity, etc. The exception is love. People can love each other and feel happy; however, you can imagine how that happiness could soon be overwhelmed by the discomfort of not having food, water, shelter, warmth, etc. Needless to say, the fact that love is a form of happiness that does not come from a good or service is not a counterpoint to the main argument, which is that humans always seek to be happier, and goods and services enable them to be happier. When a person chooses to consume a good or service, he does so because doing so would make him happier than not doing so. Therefore, in order to have a society that maximizes happiness, we need to allow humans to freely choose what goods and services they want to consume. Again, this is valid as long as the consumption of a good or service does not affect someone else. For example, one should not be free to burn a tire, as the pollution from doing so affects other people's lives.

We should clarify that free consumption of goods and services does not mean that we must consume meaninglessly and live materialistic lives. Anyone is free to do so if that is what they like. However, services like going to a concert with friends, canoeing on the lake, eating ice cream at the park, stargazing at a campsite, etc., are also options. This brings us to a good point. We know that goods and services make a person happy, but not *all* goods and *all* services make a person happy. This means that a system must be designed to ensure that the right person consumes the right goods and services. In other words, we don't want to split the goods and services in the pot exactly equally. People have different preferences, so they want to take different things out of the pot. Happiness will not be maximized if the right goods and services are not consumed by the right person.

You will see that free choice is again the best way to enable this to happen. No one other than the consumer knows exactly what he is feeling and exactly what will make him the happiest at the moment. This means that in order to ensure that the consumer's happiness is maximized, he must be the only one who decides what to consume.

We need to leave him alone, and he will naturally buy only the goods and services that make him happier. As we established earlier, a person will make a choice *only if* it makes him happier than his current state. As an example of how this works in commerce, the consumer will only trade his [$5] for [a hat] if he is happier after the exchange than before. In other words, the happiness of now owning [a hat] must outweigh the sadness of giving up [$5]. The other side of the exchange also feels the same way. The person giving up [a hat] and gaining [$5] must be happier after the trade than before; otherwise, he would not have offered to trade in the first place. You see that **every voluntary trade creates happiness as a byproduct**. Again, we know this because if it did not make both people happy to engage in the trade, the trade would not have happened. The fact that the trade did indeed happen *is proof* that both people are happier than they were before.

There is a slight caveat to this. Sometimes, trades do not increase the happiness of both parties. For example, a robbery at gunpoint is a transaction. You have exchanged [your wallet] with [nothing]. However, you are not happier after the trade than before. The simple reason for this is that the transaction is not *voluntary.* If the robber were to offer you [nothing] in exchange for [your wallet], you would normally say "no thank you." However, you have no choice but to accept the trade. It is not voluntary. In a happiness-maximizing society, all trades are free to be conducted, contingent on the fact that they are voluntary. This general principle is called: **voluntary exchange.**

If you remember, there was another example where you had no choice but to engage in a transaction; otherwise, armed people would come to your door: taxation. We see here that taxation is akin to theft. You might argue that taxation is voluntary because you do vote for it. However, it is not a unanimous vote that passes a taxation act. If 51% of the people accept a tax, it will pass, and 49% of the people will be subjected to an involuntary exchange.

The premise that all voluntary trades should be legal is hard to accept for some people due to some misconceptions about its meaning. It is important to clarify that selling harvested organs or similar gruesome transactions is not allowed. Our existing rules already make such transactions illegal. Although the seller and the buyer of the organ might be voluntarily exchanging, the same cannot be said for the person who was kidnapped. When the transaction chain is followed, we ultimately reach an involuntary transaction. Namely, the person you traded [their organ] for [nothing] at gunpoint. Involuntary transactions are illegal in our society.

We haven't yet established *what* goods and services our system will produce and *how.* These are the remaining questions society must answer, and they will be answered by the producers. In this section, we have established how the trade of those goods and services should be conducted. We have determined that since voluntary trade always makes the two parties happier, it should be encouraged as long as it affects only the two parties involved. **The people should be *free* to consume from the *market.***

The Lives Of Consumers And Producers

Let us walk through the life of a consumer. The consumer, at some point, did something for someone and **acquired some money. He has put something into the pot, and now the pot owes him ba**ck. As he is going about his day, the pot makes him offers he might want to engage in: a 2 for 1 special on t-shirts for $20, a taxi ride that will get him to his destination faster for $10, a tasty hamburger for $8. If the offers do not make him happier than he is now, he does not need to take them. Notice that the fact that there are offers that he does not want to take does not cause him any harm. He does not care about transactions that he is not a part of. At some point, if it would indeed make him happier than he is now, he picks one of these offers and trades. By doing so, he makes himself and the other party in the trade happier than they were before. The life of a consumer is simple. He only needs to think about whether he would want to or not want to take up an offer.

The life of a producer, on the other hand, is difficult. Of course, every consumer is also a producer, and vice versa, at some point, because in order for anyone to consume, they would need money. Unless they print the money, which they cannot do in our sound money society, they must have produced something for someone at some point. The producer's life is difficult because he wants the consumer's money, but the consumer does not just give it to him. The consumer wants to hold onto his money because, at some point, he also experienced what the producer is experiencing. He worked hard to get the money from someone else, and he will not give it up so easily. So the producer constantly has to come up with different goods or services that the consumer *might* like and consequently choose to exchange his money for it. The consumer is like a spoiled king, and all the producers are trying to satisfy the king's desires so that the king would just give them his money. Of course, the consumer is justified in acting in this spoiled manner because, at some point, to obtain his money, he had to satisfy a spoiled king as well. Since we already have a system that makes sure that no one consumes more than they produce, namely sound money, society guarantees that all persons do an equal amount of "desiring" and "satisfying."

Recall that we have two outstanding questions: What will society produce, and how? This synergistic relationship between producers and consumers answers these questions.

What To Produce?

First, let's explore the "What do we produce?" question. The answer is evidently: "whatever the consumer wants." A producer's only task is to satisfy the consumer. He must therefore produce whatever the consumer wants. However, notice that the consumer never actually tells the producer what he wants. The consumer just goes about his day, accepting and rejecting offers, and the producer *infers* what the consumer may want from the actions of the consumer.

Let's say a producer is in the business of making concrete shoes. His business is unsurprisingly not going great. No one wants his concrete shoes. The poor guy just wants it to be his turn to consume, but just no one would give him some money. He looks around and sees that many people are giving money to the people selling ice cream. He closes his concrete shoe business and decides to open an ice cream shop. Even though no one explicitly told the producer what they wanted, he inferred from what transactions consumers reject and which ones they accept. In other words, the market told him what to do. The ghost of the free market whispered in his ear *what to produce.*

The market is not only able to whisper about the existing goods and services. It also whispers about what new goods and services should be produced. We always hear that a free market gives way to inventions. How exactly does this happen?

The producer from the previous example initially thought that concrete shoes might be of some appeal to consumers. He was wrong, but that's okay. He is allowed to try and fail. In fact, he must be able to try and fail because no one truly knows what society wants. The individual desires of millions of people for all instances of time cannot be known. Especially for a product that does not even exist yet.

The producer, walking from one wall to the other in his room, tries to figure out just what he could produce that would make the consumer happy. What can I give to these people that would make them want to *voluntarily* hand over their money to me? He needs to go inside the consumer's mind and figure out what the consumer wants that even the consumer does not know of. The producer has an idea at some point and makes it. Then offers it to the consumer and listens. "Mmh, no," says the consumer, by rejecting the producer's offer. The producer tries again until he creates something that the consumer likes. From the consumer's perspective, everything is great as usual. He walks around rejecting and accepting offers, and the new invention of the producer is just one of these interactions. The consumer simply rejects and walks away if he does not like the product. He does not even need to apologize to the producer who poured his hard work into the product. He just goes about his day as usual. The consumer will only buy something if he is completely satisfied with it. The producer is not offended by the consumer's preferences. He keeps iterating and improving his product. One day the producer does create something consumers like and gladly collects their money.

The producer is happy with his success, but so is the consumer. Or at least he should be. He did not have to do anything, and something that he liked just came into existence. The producer becomes rich, but since the transaction was voluntary, we know that the consumer is happier after the trade than before. The producer is very rich only because he made a great number of people happy. His money represents the total amount of happiness he created. He put so much more into the pot than he took out that society owes him a great amount. That's what his money represents.

Further note that a market determines what to produce in a very decentralized way. It takes input from everyone in the market, not a central dictator that decides on everyone's behalf. If a lot of people say, inside their heads, "Hmm, you know what would be good? If

X existed," then X gets conjured into existence. And sometimes, products that people did not even think about come into existence. In this case, the producer essentially says, "You don't know that your life would be better with this, but it will be. And here, I made it for you." However, a market only works in this amazing way if it is free. If producers can try and fail freely. If they don't need a license before they do something or have to pass through millions of hoops before creating a product that solves people's problems. Therefore, as a society, **we should try to have as few regulations and licenses as possible.** Our goal should be to facilitate this synergistic relationship between producers and consumers. The principle we established for consumers applies to producers as well: Let the producers produce what they want, given that it does not affect other people. **Producers should be *free* to provide to the *market*.**

How To Produce?

The final question that remains to be determined is, "How should we produce?" This question is interlinked to the previous question. In the market, consumers accept and reject trade offers, which signal what they want to the producers so they can go make them. However, the market does not just say, "This product is good. Keep making more of it." It says, "This product is good for this price." Remember that there is always an exchange that is going on. [A product] is traded for [some money]. Ice cream makes people happy. Of course. But does it make people happier than giving up $10? Perhaps not. If you, a producer, cannot produce ice cream efficiently enough to sell it for less than $10, you should not be the one making ice cream. Your method of production is not optimal. Another producer, with a better answer to the "How to produce" question, should be the one producing ice cream. Contrastingly, if the consumers are buying ice cream at $5 from a producer, but you have a method to produce it for cheaper, which would enable you to sell it for $4, you would go ahead and do so. This would declare to all other producers that your "how to produce" method is supreme. They must either adapt or lose all their customers to you. Either way, the market is blessed with a good or service that is cheaper. Consumers are happy because they get to give up fewer pieces of money in exchange for something they like.

This time, the market again spoke in a covert way—but instead of telling us what to produce, it told us how to produce it. It again did this in a decentralized way. One central decision-maker did not declare one method of production to be better than the others. A random producer in the market found a way to create the good or service in a cheaper way than another random producer. The market then determined the cheaper production method supreme.

What drives the producer with the better method of production is **profit.** The consumers enjoyed ice cream at a lower cost because the producer with the better production method was driven by profit. He knew that if he could lower the price to $4, he could pull all the consumers toward his business and profit. The desire to profit forces prices to go down.

This is contrary to what many people think. There are many misconceptions about what leads to predatory behavior by some businesses. We should see that, although it is true that these malicious businesses do profit great amounts, it is not the fault of profit itself. Let's explore these exploitative businesses in detail to see who exactly is at fault here.

For the sake of example, suppose that the initial ice-cream seller who sold the ice cream for $5 had a profit of $0.50, meaning the cost of his rent, labor, raw materials, etc., added up to $4.50. If he decides to bump up his ice cream price to $6, trying to profit $1.50 now, a competitor will show up next to him and sell for $5, stealing all his customers. Soon, he will again need to lower his price to $5. In a free market, a business cannot exploit customers in this way. But you are skeptical of this explanation. You disagree and say that both businesses will just keep their price at $6 and exploit the customers. That is what happens in real life, right? But then why wouldn't a third ice cream seller set up next to them? If this third seller sets his price at $5.99, all the consumers would prefer him. Then, when the other two ice-cream sellers also lower their price to $5.99, the consumers will be split three ways. However, now, one of the sellers can have all the customers if he lowers his price to $5.98, so he does so. This trend continues until they hit $5. This is the price at which the profit is just enough to justify the work that the ice-cream seller is doing. The seller has to make some profit in order to sustain his business. A seller must add the smallest amount of profit that justifies to him the hassles of doing business. Otherwise, other sellers set up next to him and steal his customers.

You are likely not satisfied with this explanation because you know cases from real life that do not work like this. When the third seller arrives, he will also set his price at $6 because he is also profit-driven. The case where all sellers in a market secretly conspire like this and agree to sell at a high price is called **collusion**. And you are right. It does happen in our current society. But remember, our current society is not a free market.

What you should understand about collusion is that it is an unstable equilibrium, just like the example given before of an upside-down pyramid. Technically, if no seller breaks the balance, they can all get away with selling at $6. But it is an unstable equilibrium—because as soon as one seller cuts the price by one cent, the trajectory is downwards. A seller is always incentivized to cut prices because as soon as he cuts his price by one cent, he becomes the business preferred by all the customers. The stable equilibrium of the system is the equilibrium where all sellers sell at the lowest profit possible.

The exploitative industries of our current society exist only in unfree markets. Just like how a pyramid can remain upside down as long as something is supporting it, these exploitative industries in our current society can exist if something supports its unstable equilibrium. That means something must be preventing the force that topples an exploitative industry. As we saw in the ice cream example, the cure for an exploitative industry is the introduction of competition. What holds up the upside-down pyramid in our society is the government. If the government had said that one must obtain a license to sell ice cream, it would have prevented, discouraged, or at the least delayed the introduction of the new ice cream seller. Similarly, if the government had said that the ice cream businesses were getting too big and had created regulations for the industry, it would have made it difficult for new competition to enter the field. Even though the cure for an exploitative industry is more competition, the government does the opposite, which is to set up a bunch of hoops that businesses must jump through in order to operate. This then makes it possible for the existing businesses to become more exploitative since there is no competition to disrupt them.

It is not surprising that the healthcare industry spends the most on lobbying, multiples more than the other industries, which you can see for yourself here: https://www.opensecrets.org/federal-lobbying/industries. Make sure also to notice that pharmaceuticals, insurance, hospitals, health services, and health professionals are all shown separately. When you add them all, you get more than 7x what the oil and gas industry spends, which is an industry many don't like. If you click on one of the specific industries, you will see that there is a section for their lobbyists who are former government employees. The number for healthcare is usually between 50-60%, again hinting at the revolving door we were talking about. Healthcare is one of the most regulated industries in the U.S.

What we have seen is that the desire for profit is actually a beneficial component of the free market that encourages producers to lower prices. However, when the government puts up barriers to entry for the competition, it gives a small group of businesses the ability to profit beyond what the free market would allow them to. In other words, we just proved that provided there is no government intervention, the free market, contrary to popular belief, does not give way to companies raising prices to exploit customers but instead the opposite. It forces companies to cut prices until they reach the lowest justifiable profit amount.

But that is not all. We saw that the ice-cream sellers would *not raise* their prices to more than $5 just to profit a little extra. We will now see that the desire to profit forces all businesses actually to *lower* their prices over time. This exactly works as follows. Right now, the ice cream is sold for $5, and all costs of production come out to $4.50. A seller can pull all the customers to his business if he can lower the price by even one cent. He realizes that if he can insulate his fridge better, he can spend less on electricity and therefore make ice cream for $4.30. He cuts the final price down to $4.80, thereby drawing all the customers to him. The other businesses will go bankrupt unless they similarly cut their costs. They also insulate their fridges and lower their price to $4.80. Now the new market price for ice cream is 20 cents lower. Sometime later, another one of them realizes that he can again profit for a while until the competitors catch up if he finds a way to produce ice cream at an even lower price. Competition lowers prices, and a free market is the most competitive market. Once again, society benefits when consumers are allowed to consume freely and producers are allowed to produce freely.

The Free Market

It is now time to assemble what we learned and look at the big picture. Essentially, all consumers in a market make choices every day. These choices are just accepting or rejecting trade offers. They should be free to do so because **voluntary exchange always makes both parties happier**. The producers observe the most popular trades and estimate what the consumers might like to exchange their money for. The producers then must produce a good or service at the right price to satisfy consumers. In other words, the "what" that is created must be a desirable high-quality product, and "how" it is produced must be the most efficient way so that the price is the lowest. What drives producers to constantly try to find a cheaper way to create a high-quality product is profit. **For the system to punish collusion amongst exploitative businesses, competition is necessary.** This means that **the government should not impose barriers to entry such as regulations and licenses**. A system built on these principles is called a **free market** economy. It is when **consumers are allowed to consume freely, and the producers are allowed to produce freely, as long as doing so does not affect anyone else.**

We have thus far established that we need **sound money** and a **free market**. Now we need to decide what kind of government we want. In the next section, we will explore the actions of the government in more detail and determine what role we would like it to play in our economy.

CHAPTER 5

Government's role in the Free Market

In order to decide on the government's role in our economy, we first need to understand how the government can contribute to the economy. We need to gain an understanding of some key concepts that will help us analyze the effects that a particular government policy would have. Then, using these are newfound wisdom, we can decide whether it would be good or bad for the government to perform some particular action. So, let us get to it and see what the government's capabilities are when it comes to the economy and simultaneously clarify some common misconceptions.

Fact 1: The Government Does Not Produce Anything

Society has decided that it should take some people and give them a specific role. That role is to enact laws that would make society run better. The government is just the name for this collection of people.

So how does it work when someone says, "The government should provide X," where X is a specific good or service? As we said, the government is just a collection of people who were delegated to fulfill a certain task. That task is to write the necessary laws. They are the same exact species of humans as the rest of society. This means that they do not have magical abilities like creating goods and services from nothing. All the government does is collect money from people and spend it on things. They can spend the money they collect to buy things of value—or use the money they collect to hire contractors who produce things of value. But, the government does not fundamentally create anything itself. The people inside the government do not dedicate their labor to producing anything of value with their hands. They also cannot create goods and services from thin air.

Essentially then, the government is an entity that we created that collects money from citizens and spends it on their behalf.

Fact 2: Government Purchases Are Always Too Expensive And Low Quality

Let's begin from the ground up. Everyone on the market looking to buy something for themselves with their own money would like the most quality for the lowest price. We have the saying "Best bang for your buck" for a reason. Now, the consumer's behavior has a very logical explanation behind it. He will engage in a transaction in which he will give something he has, money, to get something else, whatever he is buying. He would like to give as little money as possible and take as much value as possible. So he naturally gravitates toward the product with the *highest value for the lowest price.*

Now imagine if our consumer was going to use someone else's money to buy himself something, and for example, assume he doesn't know or care about this someone else. What kind of product would the consumer buy? He will be the one who keeps the product— so he wants the highest quality—but he isn't giving away anything of his own in exchange since he isn't the one paying. In this case, the product purchased is a top-shelf product; *best quality, but very expensive.*

Now imagine the reverse, where he will pay for the product, but he will not be the owner of it, like a gift. Again assume that the consumer does not know who the gift recipient is and does not care about them. What kind of product will be bought under these circumstances? Now the buyer cares about the *price,* but not so much the *quality* since he won't be the one using it.

Most people feel like they would not buy the cheapest item out of decency for the gift recipient because, in real life, we only buy gifts for people we know. But imagine if the punishment for your parking ticket was to buy a gift for the parking enforcement from a menu of gifts. You would just pick the *lowest-priced item, with no regard to quality.*

Finally, the fourth case is when you spend someone else's money on a product you are not going to end up using. *Now, the buyer neither cares about the quality nor the price.* By definition, all government purchases are in this category. The government collects money from the public and spends it on things it will not end up owning. It spends other people's money on gifts for other people.

There is a counterpoint to be made here, which is that the government does care a little bit about the cost and quality of a good or service since they are also citizens, therefore partly users of the purchase, and presumably, they are also taxpayers, so partly payers for the purchase. They are also incentivized to get re-elected; however, re-election campaigning is never really about how well the tax dollars were spent. Nor do people even know what choices the government had when spending the money. People do not know whether the government made frugal choices or not. When the common person hears that the government will spend $X billion on a new bridge, they have no idea whether that is a good deal or not. Neither do they know what the government could have done with that money instead of building a bridge. Besides, all this would be extra work for a citizen, who would not only have to investigate the finances and evaluate alternatives but also spread this information to other citizens to sway the re-election outcome. Most people will just look at the bridge and say, "Wow, thank God for the government." Before the government took action, there was no bridge, and now there is one. They will not realize that before the government took action, there was $X billion, and now there is none.

Government purchases have the worst quality per dollar ratio. (Notice the keyword ratio. The quality is not necessarily the absolute lowest, not the price point the absolute highest, but their ratio is the lowest. So *per dollar paid*, the quality received is low.)

Fact 3: When The Government Spends $1 More, Citizens Get To Spend $1 Less.

Let's first take a fixed money supply as an example. In this case, for the government to spend money, it would need to tax you. So they would need to take a dollar you would spend—and spend it on your behalf. That is the only way.

The lack of understanding of this concept is worrying. It was shocking to see that governments were announcing lotteries during the COVID-19 Pandemic or straight-up money incentives to their citizens. Remember, though, the government has no money, so how would this system work? Well, you would just "win" your own taxed money back, so not exactly a payoff. Especially after considering that once you hand over the money in the first place, it goes through a bureaucratic nightmare on its way back to you, losing a chunk of it at every step.

You must understand that there is no such thing as free anything. **If the government says they will give everyone something for free, they will take money from your right pocket and put the free thing in your left pocket—but they will never point out the sleight of hand they pulled on you.** You can expect, knowing Fact 2, that the free thing will be the worst quality for the price paid. They will deceive the voters by always mentioning what they give, treating taxation as a law of nature. Voters need to stop falling for the trick of receiving a "free" 50 cents after giving away $1.

So what if the government issues bonds instead of taxing people. The basic facts don't change; only the time when the government collects the money is different. If the money is not directly taxed, it can be borrowed by issuing government bonds. In this case, the government essentially uses a credit card. Until the payment is due, everything seems to be free, but it's again just a trick. The payment date is in the future; that is the only difference. When the bond payments come due, the bills must be paid—with interest. But how? The government does not have any money of its own. So then that means higher taxes for the future citizens to pay the bills.

This is, in a sense, immoral as well because those who enjoyed the free stuff could be long dead before the bills come due. When we pay for things with debt, we enjoy ourselves now at the expense of our grandchildren. That is a problem for the future, though. Every politician only cares about the time spent when they are in office. This is why the national debt looks like this.

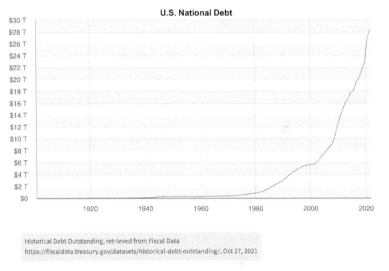

Historical Debt Outstanding, retrieved from Fiscal Data
https://fiscaldata.treasury.gov/datasets/historical-debt-outstanding/, Oct 27, 2021

Figure 5.1: National Debt nearing $30 Trillion, or $230,000 per taxpayer[4]

In the previous example, we didn't change the money supply. The government borrowed the money from an individual who wanted a bond—so the individual's money decreased precisely as much as the government's increased. But remember, the FED does something called Quantitative Easing as well. This is when they print money and loan it to the government by buying bonds.

In this case, two things can happen. Either, as the previous case went, we get taxed higher in the future to pay our debts plus interest, or what the government does now is it keeps paying its old debt with new debt. With that policy, the money supply keeps increasing but supposedly will decrease at some point in the future when we pay our debts.

But then why can't we keep printing money to pay our old debts and have newer debt? Because when the money supply increases like this forever, we get inflation, which ends up being the way we pay the bills. Inflation works as a tax the same way a sales tax works. Imagine something you always bought for $1 is now $1.10 due to inflation. The outcome is the same as a 10% sales tax. You get to buy fewer goods and services because the price of everything is higher. Government spending is always paid for one way or another. There are no "free" things that the government hands out.

For the government to spend $1 more, you must spend $1 less.

Putting It All Together

The three facts are as follows. One: the government does not produce anything; it only collects money from citizens and spends it on their behalf. Two: all government purchases are paid by others and for others to use; therefore, with no concern for quality nor price, they are of the lowest quality per price ratio. Three: there are no free things; everything that goes in your left pocket comes from your right pocket.

Combining these three ideas, one can conclude this: **It is more efficient for people to pay for their own needs—than for the government to take the money from them, pass it through layers of bureaucracy, buy something of low quality for a high price, and give it back to the people.**

Government spending is a deceptive practice that is inefficient for society. The role of the government in our economy should be as small as possible. That is, if it does not need to, it should not spend money. Previously we had decided that one of the tenets of our society should be voluntary exchange. While exploring voluntary exchange, we ruled that taxation was not a form of voluntary exchange. We should therefore minimize taxation to the lowest amount we can. Now with the newly established principle of **limited government**, this should not be such a problem.

Until this point, we also made small comments about the certain laws that would exist in our society. We said, for example, that regulations and licensing laws should be minimal. We also said that voluntary exchanges that affect third parties could be regulated, and of course, all involuntary exchanges as well. Let us now again start from basic principles and define the laws of our society. Now, in more detail.

CHAPTER 6

What Laws Should We Have?

The Foundation For Our Laws

The new laws in a society are built upon earlier laws, which were built upon even earlier laws. Since we are starting from scratch, we need to come up with the first law. It must be based upon a truth; otherwise, all other laws which will be driven from the central law will be false. Therefore, our first task is to discover a true statement upon which we can build our laws.

Finding this truth is not as easy as it sounds. Most people would agree that math is a useful skill and that people should know how to do basic addition and subtraction. But should this be the fundamental truth that we place at the center of our society? Or, consider another example. We all know the long-term harms that smoking cigarettes can cause. Although many would agree that people should not smoke, can this be a foundational principle?

The issue is that "one must know math" and "one must not smoke" are neither fundamental nor true. They are not fundamental because they are derived from other principles. "One must know math" is true only to a person who assumes that "one must have useful skills," and "one must not smoke" is only true to a person who assumes that "one must be healthy." Is it true that one must be healthy? And how do you even define "health?" Maybe you prefer the short-term happiness of smoking to the long-term happiness of being healthy. How do you define a "useful skill?" And, who says that you should have useful skills? Maybe you prefer playing games over learning skills.

You see, it is hard to come up with a principle that does not derive its truth from other principles. But you see that we do need such a principle because we need something from which we base all laws in our society. A society that cannot do so is a society built on false premises, which means that all its laws will be void. We must point at something when asked why such and such law is a good law. When you trace back the origin of any law, you must eventually come to some fact that does not derive its truth from anything else. It is just true by default. Its evidence should be itself: it should be **self-evident**.

The principle that we will base our society on is **self-ownership.** The fundamental statement that you must accept as true is: "You, and only you, own yourself." When creating something from nothing, you must accept at least one thing to be true without proof because, at the point of conception, there is nothing to base the first truth off of. This is that truth. It is the axiom of our society. You are, of course, free to reject the axiom. In which case, none of the laws that follow from this simple axiom will be valid to you either. However, it is unlikely that you will reject the axiom of our society. Doing so would imply that someone else owns you. That means that someone can tell you to do something, and you must do it against your will. It means that your life belongs to someone else and that you are not the decision-maker in your own life. It means that someone else owns the rights to your body. From this point on, it will be assumed that you have accepted the axiom that people in our society are the owners of their lives.

The first law that we can immediately conclude from this is that murder is not allowed. If you own your life, then no one can take it from you. Taking other people's lives is illegal. That is the definition of murder.

You cannot take the entirety of one's life from them; however, what about just a portion of their lives. Can you take just two years of someone's life? Of course, if people own their lives, then you cannot take small chunks of their lives either. So that means you cannot lock someone in a room for two years. You cannot kidnap someone. You cannot, in general, make someone do something against their will. Since people own their lives, they get to choose what they would like to do with their lives. By making them do something against their will, you are taking away a chunk of their life.

This ability of people to do as they wish has a name: **liberty.** Liberty means that you are free to choose your actions. No one else can make you do something which you do not want to. But how do we actually know whether someone actually makes a choice because they want to or because someone else is forcing them to? How do we know that there indeed is liberty in our society? The answer brings us to the principle of **voluntarism.** As we established earlier, if an action is done purely voluntarily, it must mean that the actor has increased his internal happiness by doing so. You see that an earlier principle we established for our economy, voluntary exchange, makes its way into our legal framework as well. In addition to voluntary exchanges in commerce, we now establish that all actions in our society must also be voluntary.

We reasoned that no one could take away a chunk of your life. To explore this idea further, visualize your life as a loaf of sliced bread. One end of the bread is the time of your birth, and the other end is the time of your death. Right now, let's say that you are right in the middle of the loaf of bread. To kidnap and lock you in a basement for two years would be analogous to taking away two years worth of slices from your future. To murder would be analogous to taking away all the slices. What about taking away the slices which you have already lived through? Say if you are currently 30 years old, should someone be able to take years 26 through 28 from you? And how exactly would they even do this since you have already lived those years? Regardless of how one would go about this action, we can agree that it should not be allowed. It does not matter whether you take away future slices, past slices, or all slices; taking slices is just illegal.

So what does taking past slices look like? Well, as you go through life, you pour your life into the things you do. Things you create during your life are the physical manifestations of a chunk of your life. For example, if during the ages of 26 through 28, you built a house, that house now represents a two-year chunk of your life. Meaning that if one were to take that house away from you, they would be taking away a portion of your life. They would be taking the slices of bread between the ages of 26 through 28. Therefore, in our society, people are not allowed to take away the things that others create. Since people own their lives, you own their labor as well. They own the work that they do during their lives. This logic holds for the things that you may trade your house for as well. If you voluntarily exchange the house you built for a car, you now own that car. It is illegal for anyone to take away that car from you. It is your **private property**: a physical manifestation of a chunk of your life or something you traded a chunk of your life for. Taking away one's property is illegal for the exact same reason that murder and kidnapping are illegal. Murder and theft are not unrelated crimes. They are different magnitudes of the same type of crime. Theft is micro-murder.

So what we know so far is that no one else has power over you but yourself. You have **liberty.** No one can take away the potential future actions you will perform with this liberty, so you have a right to **life.** The same applies to your past; therefore, no one can take away your **property.** You may choose to trade anything you own **voluntarily.** What breaks voluntarism is aggression or a threat of aggression. For our society to be based on voluntarism as we would like, there needs to be no aggression. We can call this the **Non-Aggression Principle**. The Non-Aggression Principle, or NAP, is such a comprehensive law that we are done. We do not need any more laws. Every particular action that people can take relates to the NAP.

Besides obvious examples of aggression like punching, raping, and murdering, the NAP prevents things like vandalism. Spraypainting one's car is an act of aggression against their property, which is their life. Polluting the air is also an act of aggression against property. Air is a commodity that we all own. It is the property of everyone. You also cannot yell into someone's ear. By doing so, you would be essentially aggressing by hitting them with powerful pressure waves. You see that we can go on like this and define all further laws from the NAP. By having a core principle that all our laws derive from, we make the rules of our society easy to know and follow. One does not need to read through the 70,000+ pages of the federal law books to know whether an action is allowed. If it violates the NAP, it's not allowed. If it doesn't, it is allowed.

The Role Of Government

Perfect. We have created the necessary principle that all laws can derive from, the Non-Aggression Principle, and it is founded on a rock-solid, self-evident truth that people own themselves. Now we need a government to enforce these laws. That should be the only job of the government. It should solely intervene in cases where the NAP is violated.

How will the government enforce laws? Clearly, a law-breaker is not listening to instructions because then they wouldn't be breaking the laws in the first place. You cannot just say "don't" to a murderer. The law already said, "don't," but the murderer did not listen. Something else must be done. What the government can do is take away things that the law-breaker owns.

First, it should begin by taking away property. This is what a fine is. You must pay $10,000 when caught littering, for example. For more serious crimes, more property can be taken away. If a crime is so severe, more than property must be taken away: liberty. This means jail. If a very serious law is broken, the law-breaker will be put in jail, thereby losing his liberty. And some places have given their government the power to take away the only thing that remains once property and liberty are taken: life. This would be the death penalty. Taking away one's liberty for a long time essentially means taking away their life, but the death penalty permanently does this. Since judgments can always be incorrect, the government should not take away life. Plus, giving the state the power to execute people is a dangerous line to cross. However, sometimes, like in active-terrorist situations, that line must be crossed. The government's troops on the street, in other words, the police, must de-escalate the terror situation and might need to take the life of the terrorist if the lives of other people are in danger.

Notice that in our society, the government is the only one allowed to take away life, liberty, and property. *We* give it this power. We want to give this power to the government because we trust that it will use it only when our life, liberty, and property are in danger. That is, the government will *not* use its power to take away *our* lives, liberties, and properties—but instead, it will *use it to ensure that bad people do not* take our lives, liberties, or properties. We give these special powers to the government to *protect* our life, liberty, and property. However, we do not forget that these special powers we hand over to the government have the potential for abuse. We keep a close eye on the government and make sure that it does not deviate from its designated purpose. And if it does so, we swiftly take corrective measures to ensure that a government that is true to its purpose is in place again.

Putting It All Together

Let's see an overview of our laws and the role of our government in this society. We started with a **self-evident** statement that only we own ourselves. From this, we concluded that we also own our **life, liberty, and property.** These are the fundamental rights that all people in our society have. We are **equal** in this regard. No one can take away anyone else's life, liberty, or property. **These rights are unalienable**. The only exception is the government. **For the sole purpose of securing these rights**, a government is instituted amongst us. This government has special powers to fulfill its job, but **it derives these powers from us**. It relies on **our consent** to exercise the power it has. If the government does become abusive of its powers, **we have the right to apply corrective measures or abolish it completely** and institute a new government based again on **our fundamental principles.**

If we were to write this in an older form of English, it might read like this:

> *"We hold these truths to be self-evident, that all men are created equal, that they are endowed by their Creator with certain unalienable Rights, that among these are Life, Liberty and the pursuit of Happiness.—That to secure these rights, Governments are instituted among Men, deriving their just powers from the consent of the governed,—That whenever any Form of Government becomes destructive of these ends, it is the Right of the People to alter or to abolish it, and to institute new Government, laying its foundation on such principles and organizing its powers in such form, as to them shall seem most likely to affect their Safety and Happiness."*

This is the Declaration of Independence of the United States. You see, this society that we have been building all along is not so different than the United States of America. That is, the old U.S.A., where the government was not abusive of its powers. There was sound money and free markets. And all laws were based on the fundamentally solid principle of self-ownership.

The United States of America was founded by people who understood the dangers of oppressive governments. The founders understood that the more power the government has, the less power the people have. They knew that the worst threat to human life historically had been authoritarian governments. For these reasons, they placed the foundations of the country on liberty. This is why France gave the Statue of Liberty only to the United States.

The United States was lucky. It is not often that one gets to create a country from scratch. But because of this fact, Americans enjoyed true freedom. Unlike other countries that gained some freedom from a powerful monarch, Americans started out free. A government was created only in order to ensure that the people remained free. The difference is worth emphasizing. In other countries, people were permitted by the ruling class to have some freedom after rebelling; in America, people had all their freedoms from the onset and permitted the government to have some abilities. It was the only place where *the people* truly had the power. What led from that was the greatest prosperity the world had ever seen. Millions from around the world rushed to America because there they were free. There, they could pursue their dreams and live as they wished. Liberty was what turned a little colony of an empire into a country that now has a GDP that is multiple times that of the former empire.

America has turned out to be a successful experiment that free individuals can govern themselves better than any ruling class can and generate more prosperity than ever before. It is evidence of the fact that the society we have been building in this book from scratch does, in fact, work in real life. As the people of the world, we are lucky that history has played out in a way that led to the creation of America. It shows that we all can, and in fact, we all must be free.

The same freedom that made America the most prosperous economy can be applied worldwide to maximize the productive capabilities of the world. This should be the goal of the world simply because we must make the most out of our limited resources. Doing so enables us to survive better. Therefore, we *must* produce as efficiently as we can, especially if we want to help the poorest amongst us. Prosperity benefits all humankind.

CHAPTER 7

Decentralized Governence

In the society we built from scratch, we instituted a government only to preserve the rights of the people. We gave this government special powers to ensure that a fellow citizen's life, liberty, and property are not infringed upon. These special powers automatically made the government stronger than all the citizens; however, we had no choice but to do this. We needed an entity stronger than a particular citizen so that he may be stopped when he violates the rights of other citizens. Our problem now is to ensure that this stronger entity, namely the government, never violates the rights of a fellow citizen. In other words, we must make sure that the government stays true to its purpose.

We must clearly write down the rules that the government must abide by. This rule book will confine the special powers given to the government and therefore guarantee the rights of the people. Notice the difference between what we are creating here to what you might see in a classic society. We are not creating a rulebook for the people. Our society is based on liberty. We are creating a rule book for the government. Of course, the entire reason we need the government is to ultimately legislate some rules that we, the people, will follow, but from the onset, we tell the government what restrictions it may impose on us.

The government is like a powerful monster that we occasionally need to use to stop a citizen from violating the rights of another. The rulebook we will make is a cage for the beast. We can expand or shrink the cage when needed by adjusting the rulebook, but we cannot completely let the monster out of its cage. An unhinged monster will soon violate our rights, which would be the opposite of our intentions behind creating the monster in the first place.

Monopoly Of Violence

Let us resurface a question we asked before: What happens if you don't pay your taxes? Maybe you will get a letter first. What if you ignore that letter? Then you get another letter or some fines. What if you don't take those seriously either? Maybe they will send an agent to your house. What if you don't open the door? Well, then strong people with guns break into your home. What if you still don't comply? Then you either get shot, tased, or assaulted in some way and put in handcuffs. The point of this example is to illustrate again that every law is backed up by force. All forms of enforcement stem from violence. Try another example yourself. Just keep asking what would happen if the citizen repeatedly does not comply with the requests. At the end of the road, there is always some form of violence. It has to be this way because there is no other way to force someone to do something which they do not want to do.

The police and other arms of the government, specifically for the U.S., the SWAT teams, National Guard, FBI, ATF, DEA, IRS, etc., are all there to keep you in check with threats of violence if you resist. Authoritarians from history know this well.

> *"All political power comes from the barrel of a gun. The communist party must command all the guns, that way, no guns can ever be used to command the party."*
>
> – MAO ZEDONG

> *"One man with a gun can control 100 without one."*
>
> – VLADIMIR ILYICH LENIN

A good definition of a state is a "monopoly on violence." Each person living in a state has some "violence units" since, at the very least, they can punch. Maybe some individuals have a knife or a gun. But these are no match for the state, which owns most of the "violence units." For example, it has an armed police force that enforces the state's laws on the streets. No other entity besides the state has a gang of armed men patrolling the streets. No single person's violence capability exceeds the state's violence capability. This precisely is why laws are able to be enforced at all. For an entity to enact its laws, it must have the most "violence units." Otherwise, there is no reason for a law-breaker to cease his actions. He who has all the guns sets all the rules. That is just the way it is. Let's hold on to this fact for a minute.

Strategy 1: Create Alternative Monopolies Of Violence

In our society based on liberty, we do not want the state to rule over us in unwanted ways using its monopoly of violence. However, we do want the state to enforce the proper laws that we deem necessary to secure our rights. You see, it is such a challenge to balance the power that must be given to the government. It must be just enough to enforce the necessary laws but not too much to get tyrannical. Maintaining this balance is critical for society.

But how can you set up a government with the perfect amount of power in a constantly changing world? Just like how a bicycle rider must actively steer left or right to keep the bicycle balanced on varying terrain, the government must actively adjust its policies to run society well in a dynamic world. We cannot set policies in stone and expect them to hold out till eternity. Society must be actively managed.

So then the question is, who? Who knows how to run the government perfectly? Who can maintain the balance between tyranny and securing rights the best? We don't know. However, we don't need to know as long as we have options and the ability to choose between them freely. If we had fifty mini-countries inside one country, we could let the fifty different governments experiment with their unique governing methods. We could then look and see which government maintains the best balance. We can carry this one step further and create several counties with their own governments within those mini-countries. You can probably see what this is hinting at. If the mini-countries are called states, their unification would be called the United States. From the top-down, the governments would be the federal government, state governments, and county governments.

We have achieved two things by dividing a country into smaller mini-countries like this. First, we divided the monopoly of violence into fifty smaller monopolies. Then, within those monopolies, we created even smaller monopolies called counties. This way, the danger of having one big center of power that could easily turn tyrannical is mitigated. Second, we found a good way to solve the balancing problem. That is, how to balance the power of the government so that it remains on the thin line between securing rights and violating rights. The solution is to run fifty experiments and let the people freely choose amongst them. Furthermore, let one choose amongst the many counties within one of the states. In effect, we have given the people the right to choose which entity will rule over them.

The second point should remind us of how the free market finds the best answer to a question. No one person knows what to produce and how to produce these things, but in a free market, people are free to experiment and see if other people like their solutions. Time has shown that this approach is superior to appointing a central planner who would decide how to combine the resources to produce what. Now, when answering the question of how to govern, we can reason that giving the governments a chance to experiment and the people the right to choose would also be an excellent method to find the best answer.

Strategy 2: Use The Lowest Government Possible

Our first strategy was to have many smaller centers of power rather than one big one. The second strategy will be to say that every law should be instigated at the lowest form of government possible. Taking the U.S. as an example, this would mean that if the residents of Florida would like to implement a speed limit near school zones, they may do so using their state government. This law does not need to be a federal law. In fact, if only the residents of Miami want this law, it does not need to be a state law either. But why exactly do we prefer lower governments to higher ones?

First of all, there is a high degree of agreement amongst the locals of a region. Within a local town, there will be plenty of issues that at least 90% of the people agree on, but there are just a handful of issues that 90% of all members of a country would agree on. Furthermore, there are only a few issues, like national defense, that concern the entire country. Most of the problems can be solved locally without bothering the other people in the country. Most importantly, we do not want anyone living in one region to impose rules upon another region. In the end, the goal of Strategy 1 was to give every citizen the right to choose which rules they would like to live under. What good is having multiple governments if they all have the same laws?

Second, the lower governments must always be more accountable to their people. A county government can only mistreat its people to an extent. This is because the county government's jurisdiction is confined to certain geographic borders. The people of an abusive county government are free to move out of the county government's jurisdiction and into a county with a better government. This maintains a check on the county governments. Notice that this is also true for the state governments, but to a lesser extent. You may indeed move out of one state and into another, but this is not such an easy task. Therefore, state governments can be more abusive before their citizens "vote with their feet" and leave the state. Although it is hard to move out of state, the availability of alternatives still keeps a check on the states. The federal government is barely accountable to the people. Leaving the country is not an option for many and should not be something the citizens must do to preserve their liberty.

We may thus conclude that we want the federal government to do very little because it is the least accountable to the people. The state governments should do more, but still less than the county governments. As we go up the levels of government, our ability to attend meetings and express concerns is diminished, and the option to relocate becomes more difficult. In addition, the level of agreement decreases as more people with different values get grouped under larger governments. This is why all laws should be legislated in the lowest form of government possible.

The rulebook of the United States, called the Constitution, actually already has this law. It is called the Tenth Amendment, and it is as follows:

> "The powers not delegated to the United States by the Constitution, nor prohibited by it to the States, are reserved to the States respectively, or to the people."

We can copy this directly into our rulebook.

Strategy 3: Enumerate The Powers Of The Federal Government

Implicit in the Tenth Amendment, which we just adopted, is another defense against tyranny. Let's read this simple sentence more carefully. It says that "The powers not delegated to the United States by the Constitution," meaning to the federal government, "are reserved to the States" or "to the people," as long as the Constitution does not prohibit that power. So, the federal government only has the powers delegated to it in the Constitution, and the states and the people have all the powers that are not prohibited by the Constitution.

This is a good strategy that we should adopt as well. We can write the following:

The federal government by default does not have a certain power unless the rulebook explicitly says so, and the state governments and the people by default do have a certain power unless the rulebook explicitly says it does not.

We go to great lengths to limit the federal government because it is the most dangerous government since it is the least accountable and the most powerful. However, we cannot get rid of it entirely because the states do need to coordinate certain things as a union. Therefore, we need to very clearly limit its power. We cannot just stop with Strategy 2 and say that every law should be created at the lowest form of government. We know that governments tend towards corruption, and the federal government being the most powerful and the least accountable, will be corrupted easily. So Strategy 3 is vital.

In our rulebook, we need to explicitly define the federal government's powers and ban the states from doing certain things. Then, we need to make sure that the federal powers are not up to interpretation. America suffers a great deal today because the federal powers given by the Constitution are misinterpreted, even though the intentions of the founders are crystal clear to anyone who reads the document.

A Deeper Dive Into The Current Situation In America

The United States states explicitly defines the powers of its federal government in Article 1 Section 8 of the U.S. Constitution:

> *"The Congress shall have Power To lay and collect Taxes, Duties, Imposts and Excises, to pay the Debts and provide for the common Defence and general Welfare of the United States; but all Duties, Imposts and Excises shall be uniform throughout the United States;*
>
> *To borrow Money on the credit of the United States;*
>
> *To regulate Commerce with foreign·Nations, and among the several States, and with the Indian Tribes;*
>
> *To establish an uniform Rule of Naturalization, and uniform Laws on the subject of Bankruptcies throughout the United States;*
>
> *To coin Money, regulate the Value thereof, and of foreign Coin, and fix the Standard of Weights and Measures;*
>
> *To provide for the Punishment of counterfeiting the Securities and current Coin of the United States;*
>
> *To establish Post Offices and post Roads;*
>
> *To promote the Progress of Science and useful Arts, by securing for limited Times to Authors and Inventors the exclusive Right to their respective Writings and Discoveries;*
>
> *To constitute Tribunals inferior to the supreme Court;*
>
> *To define and punish Piracies and Felonies committed on the high Seas, and Offences against the Law of Nations;*

To declare War, grant Letters of Marque and Reprisal, and make Rules concerning Captures on Land and Water;

To raise and support Armies, but no Appropriation of Money to that Use shall be for a longer Term than two Years;

To provide and maintain a Navy;

To make Rules for the Government and Regulation of the land and naval Forces;

To provide for calling forth the Militia to execute the Laws of the Union, suppress Insurrections and repel Invasions;

To provide for organizing, arming, and disciplining, the Militia, and for governing such Part of them as may be employed in the Service of the United States, reserving to the States respectively, the Appointment of the Officers, and the Authority of training the Militia according to the discipline prescribed by Congress;

To exercise exclusive Legislation in all Cases whatsoever, over such District (not exceeding ten Miles square) as may, by Cession of particular States, and the Acceptance of Congress, become the Seat of Government of the United States, and to exercise like Authority over all Places purchased by the Consent of the Legislature of the State in which the Same shall be, for the Erection of Forts, Magazines, Arsenals, dock-Yards, and other needful Buildings;–And

To make all Laws which shall be necessary and proper for carrying into Execution the foregoing Powers, and all other Powers vested by this Constitution in the Government of the United States, or in any Department or Officer thereof."

As you can see, the federal government has just eighteen powers delegated to it. The rest of the power is supposed to lie with the states and the people. However, the federal government is bigger than ever, with no indication of slowing down, and the majority of the country wants even more power delegated to it. Americans try to solve all their problems at the federal level these days, then complain that the government is not representative of them. All the while, the solution is in plain sight: the Constitution.

But why then is it not enforced? It is. The Supreme Court misinterprets the phrase "general welfare" to mean basically anything the federal government wants. For example, the Department of Education is an unconstitutional federal agency. Certainly, if a state wishes to create a Department of Education for itself, it may do so. However, this should not be a federal matter. The eighteen enumerated powers include the ability to establish post offices, maintain a navy, and provide for the nation's common defense. Are these not "general welfare" as well. Why explicitly list the federal government's powers if "general welfare" means everything? Why have the Tenth Amendment?

Another misinterpreted clause is, "[The Congress shall have the power] To regulate Commerce with foreign Nations, and among the several States, and with the Indian Tribes." The federal government takes this to mean it can regulate all commerce. The Constitution says that the federal government can regulate commerce amongst the states and with foreign nations. This makes sense because commerce amongst several States might necessitate a governing body that would unite the states. Similarly, when transacting with foreign nations, the states might need to act in a unified fashion. However, broad sweeping regulation of all commerce by the federal government would clearly be contradictory to the liberty of the states.

If the Constitution was respected, commerce, in general, would not be regulated by a federal government. When the states want to themselves, they could instigate specific laws. But the federal government would remain a powerful tool that would be used rarely. If the states are able to handle the problem, they ought to do so without the federal government's reach.

As further evidence of how the Constitution is supposed to be interpreted, let's read the words of James Madison, one of the Founding Fathers:

> "The powers delegated by the proposed Constitution to the federal government, are few and defined. Those which are to remain in the State governments are numerous

and indefinite. The former will be exercised principally on external objects, as war, peace, negotiation, and foreign commerce; with which last the power of taxation will, for the most part, be connected."

The federal government should only be needed in a few cases involving the interests of the entirety of the United States, such as "war, peace, negotiation, and foreign commerce," which James Madison summarizes as "external objects." This makes sense since these external objects are of concern to all the citizens. He further elaborates that the power of taxation will, for the most part, be connected to these issues. Today, the federal government taxes a tremendous amount, much more than the states, and involves itself in almost every aspect of our lives. Its powers do not appear to be "few and defined" by any standard.

"The powers reserved to the several States will extend to all the objects which, in the ordinary course of affairs, concern the lives, liberties, and properties of the people, and the internal order, improvement, and prosperity of the State."

It is very clear that the states should be the ones involved in affairs concerning "the lives, liberties, and properties of the people, and the internal order, improvement, and prosperity," not the federal government. The states are given "numerous and indefinite" powers to do so, as opposed to the limited powers of the federal government. If Americans respect the Tenth Amendment, they may once again have a government that is accountable to them.

Finally, let's look at the Eighteenth Amendment and the Twenty-First Amendment. They stand as proof of the decentralization of power that is instilled into the core of the United States. During the entire existence of the United States, there have only been twenty-seven amendments, and two of these were dedicated to alcohol. The Eighteenth Amendment bans the manufacturing, sale, and transportation of intoxicating liquids, and the Twenty-First Amendment repeals the Eighteenth Amendment.

Section 1 of the Eighteenth Amendment:

"After one year from the ratification of this article the manufacture, sale, or transportation of intoxicating liquors within, the importation thereof into, or the exportation thereof from the United States and all territory subject to the jurisdiction thereof for beverage purposes is hereby prohibited."

Section 1 of the Twenty-First Amendment:

"The eighteenth article of amendment to the Constitution of the United States is hereby repealed."

Passing an amendment to the Constitution is no easy task. However, it was done so because, in the past, the people still respected the Constitution and understood that the Constitution binds the federal government. The only way to ban alcohol in the entire United States would be by using the federal government's power. Therefore the document that gives the federal government its power, the Constitution, had to be amended.

Long past is the era in which a two-thirds majority had to be congregated to amend the Constitution and give the federal government a specific power. Today, the federal government is bigger and more powerful than ever. It controls every aspect of Americans' lives—with no regard to the document that confines its powers.

We should notice from this that the real-world country, which ranks the most similar to the society we have been crafting, evidenced by the Declaration of Independence, is currently far from its constitutional principles. The lesson to take is that the interpretation of the document will change with time. Governments will slowly be corrupted, and the effects will compound onto one another. As the government gains power, it will be able to influence how the document that confines its power is interpreted. The Constitution is clear to those who want to read it with genuine intent. It is crystal clear when combined with the founders' writings from outside of the Constitution. However, those with malicious intentions will always be able to find something between the lines. Our constitution must therefore be impossible to misinterpret.

Strategy 4: Nullification

Strategy 2 was to use the lowest possible form of government to create a law. Strategy 4 is to use the lowest form of government to enforce any law. Ideally, Strategy 2 will work, and there will not be any overreaching laws from higher governments. However, if there is, then Strategy 4 will be there to protect the people from living under unfavorable laws.

As an example, let's use California. Although cannabis is a Schedule 1 regulated substance according to the federal government, the State of California does not enforce this federal law and effectively voids that specific federal law. The citizens of California have decided that cannabis laws are not necessary to protect their safety and happiness and therefore choose not to enforce them. A lower form of government can invalidate a law from a higher form of government and restore the liberty of its citizens.

Strategy 4 relies on the ability of lower governments to stand up to the higher governments. If the federal government abuses its power, the states can deprive it of power by choosing not to enforce some particular law. This is the process of nullification. Similarly, the local governments can nullify state laws. This brings about one question. What if the local governments become abusive? Is there a lower form of government that can stand up to the local government?

Yes. Each individual is a government of one. Just like how states have the power to stand up to the federal government and how local governments have the power to stand up to the state governments, individuals must ultimately have the power to stand up to their local governments. Don't forget that the people are the creators of the government. And, we saw in the Declaration of Independence that if the governments that we created no longer secure our rights, if they no longer derive their just powers from the consent of the governed, then it is the right of the people to alter or abolish that government, and to institute a new government.

Here is the Declaration of Independence once again for reference:

> *"We hold these truths to be self-evident, that all men are created equal, that they are endowed by their Creator with certain unalienable Rights, that among these are Life, Liberty and the pursuit of Happiness.—That to secure these rights, Governments are instituted among Men, deriving their just powers from the consent of the governed,—That whenever any Form of Government becomes destructive of these ends, it is the Right of the People to alter or to abolish it, and to institute new Government, laying its foundation on such principles and organizing its powers in such form, as to them shall seem most likely to affect their Safety and Happiness."*

The Declaration of Independence may state that it is the right of the people to stand up to their governments, but it does not say anything about how. How will the people have the power to stand up to governments? Remember our earlier discussion about how every law is enforced. Since all laws are ultimately enforced at gunpoint:

> *"the right of the people to keep and bear arms, shall not be infringed."*

In the United States, this is called the Second Amendment. It fits into our society as the last piece that decentralizes the power of the government to the furthest extent possible. It is a backup for when all other methods fail.

It is not absurd to think that the situation would ever come down to this. Only 80 years ago, which is the duration of just one human lifetime, Germany, the powerhouse of Europe today, rallied up 6 million Jews and killed them. Societies can change very quickly. Germans are not any more barbaric than the rest of us. They are the same brand of Homo Sapiens as us. There is no reason to be so confident that our society would never do such a thing. All our other rights depend on the right to bear arms. Without it, society would lose its decentralized governance and pave the way for an abusive government.

In conclusion, Strategy 4 is to delegate the enforcement of laws to the lowest form of government possible, but we saw that it depends on the right to bear arms. It is a necessary condition for a safe society that the government must have a majority of the "violence units." Its "violence units" must be greater than that of law-breakers. However, the "violence units" of *united* individuals must be greater than that of the government. This is how society can maintain the balance between protecting rights and violating rights.

CHAPTER 8

Funding The Government

We are almost done creating the government for our society. We derived the laws it must enforce from basic principles. Then, we decentralized its power to maintain the balance between protecting rights and violating rights. The final thing we must do is fund this government.

In Chapter 5, we arrived at some facts about the government. We understood that essentially, the government is an entity that we created that collects money from citizens and spends it on their behalf. It does not create anything itself. The government just takes money from people and pays other people to create something. This means that it spends other people's money on something other people will use. Therefore, it is highly inefficient.

We can quickly see why this is true again. Say you have to buy a toaster as a wedding gift. You would buy, or at least you would prefer to buy, the cheapest toaster if you didn't care about being rude, of course. Since you are not the user of the toaster, you have little regard for its quality. Alternatively, if you won a competition and were given a limitless credit card to buy a toaster, you would buy the highest quality toaster, regardless of its price. Since you are not the payer of the toaster, you have little regard for its price. Now, since the government always spends other people's money on goods and services for other people, its purchases are always low quality per price.

Finally, we saw that the only way for the government to spend $1 is to have you not spend $1 less. That is, the government cannot create something from nothing. When it spends money, that money ultimately comes from the people. The only question is how. If it is taxed, the connection is clear. $1 is taken from you and given to the government. If it is borrowed, $1 is taken from you, and in exchange, a promise for a future $1, plus interest, is given. So today, it seems like the government just has created $1 out of nothing, but the caveat is that the future people will be taxed $1, plus the interest, to fulfill the promise. Again, no free lunch. Finally, if the future people are not taxed to pay the promise, the money will be printed. Then the price of everything goes up, which behaves the same way as a tax, just more deceptive. Instead of openly taking $1 from your stack of $11, the government goes behind your back and creates inflation that causes the price of everything to go up by 10%.

We see that there is nothing extra to be gained from the government spending money. The money ultimately comes from the people. In fact, since the government is inefficient and its purchases have low quality per price ratio, it is better for the government not to spend money. The government should spend the least amount of money possible.

This especially holds true for the federal government. Power and money go hand in hand. For the power to be decentralized, spending must be close to the people. Power is, by definition, the ability to do work in a given amount of time. Money is necessary for the execution of power because it enables work to be done. By keeping the money in the lower forms of government, we can maintain the decentralization of power. By default, people hold their money. If it is to be spent by a government, precedence is given to lower governments.

Having established these rules, let's now try to figure out how to fund the government. That is, we know government spending ultimately comes from us, but let's decide how we should go about it. Perhaps, the U.S. Constitution could come in handy again. Let's see what their approach was.

Money Printing In The United States

First of all, there are three ways to spend: tax, borrow, and print. However, any money borrowed will ultimately be paid back with either taxed or printed dollars. Therefore there are really only two ways to fund the government.

Let's first look at printing money. We already went through how it is not fair because it gives the early spenders the ability to steal from the later spenders. This has drastic effects on inequality. What we didn't talk about is how deceptive it is.

To start off, it fools the public into thinking that government spending comes for free when in reality, we know that the bill just comes to the people later via inflation. It paves the way for the government to increase its power because the people are under the illusion that if the government does something, it's free. The truth is the opposite. If the government decides to pay for something and provide it for free, you can be assured that the taxpayers are paying a whole lot more than if they were to buy it themselves without the government in the way.

Second, it dissociates the government from the decrease in purchasing power that the public experiences. When the government taxes, people directly see their dollars decrease. However, when money is printed, people hold the same number of dollars, but those dollars are now less valuable. The dollars buy less stuff because the price of everything went up. The government then blames this inflation on the "greedy corporations."

The case against money printing is clear. As we established before, we want sound money in our system. But when reading the 18 enumerated power, you may have noticed that the federal government has the power "To coin Money, regulate the Value thereof, and of foreign Coin, and fix the Standard of Weights and Measures." Knowing the importance of sound money for a free and fair society, you may be confused about how the Constitution can give the government the power to print money. The answer is that it doesn't. To coin money does not mean to print money. The money at the time of the Founding Fathers was sound.

The transition from sound money to fiat money was explained before. We first went from using literal gold coins exchanging hands to gold stored with a trusted custodian. The custodian would issue gold deposit receipts, which the people could trade. Then Nixon broke the tie of the gold deposit receipts from gold, hence creating money backed by faith only, in other words, fiat money.

We also went over the issues with using gold, one being the difficulty of verifying the legitimacy of the gold coin received. To solve this problem, one could take their gold to a trusted entity with a unique mold or stamp, who will then create a gold coin for them. Now the people who trust this entity will recognize the special design on the coin and trust that it is real gold. This is called coining. A specialist verifies the legitimacy of the gold and makes a coin out of it so other parties in the market can comfortably accept the gold.

The Constitution just says that the federal government can act as this coiner. It might be something the federal government would like to do because commerce would be difficult if the coins people used were all from different mints with different weights. This is why it can "regulate the Value thereof, and of foreign Coin, and fix the Standard of Weights and Measures."

As further evidence that the United States should be using sound money, we can look at Article 1 Section 10:

> *"No State shall...make any Thing but gold and silver Coin a Tender in Payment of Debts."*

Now, this is a rule imposed on the states. There is no similar statement for the federal government. However, remember what James Madison said. The federal government has "few and defined" powers. Issuing fiat currency is not amongst the eighteen powers defined. If the constitution does not explicitly give the federal government the power to do something, it cannot do it by default. On the contrary, the powers delegated to the states are "numerous and indefinite." The states have the power to do what they want by default unless the constitution explicitly bans it. Therefore, the states need to be explicitly banned from issuing fiat currency, but the federal government is never even given the power to do so.

We know about the devastating effects of fiat money. It is fundamentally a tool that benefits the issuer of the currency and hurts the ones forced to accept it. If anything is to be understood from the Constitution, it would be that the intention is to protect the people. The document clearly aims to limit the power of government. It would make absolutely no sense for the Constitution to give the government the immense power to issue fiat money.

Taxation In The United States

The other option is taxation. We also went over why taxation is not fair. It clearly violates the voluntary exchange principle we established. We reasoned that involuntarily taking one's money is equivalent to murdering a fraction of their life since people accumulate money by pouring their life into work. However, taxation, and this is in no way suggesting that it is moral, is preferable to money printing. In the end, if the government is to do something, it needs to get this money somehow. Taxation is a direct, honest way of doing it instead of the indirect, deceptive practice of money printing.

When the people in society directly hand over their money to the government, they demand that the government be accountable. There is a backlash when taxes rise. No one enjoys signing a check and mailing it to the government by hand every year for their cut of your labor or paying more for a product because of the added sales tax. The U.S. does a good job at adding the tax at the very end, right when you are checking out, which serves as a reminder that a portion of this transaction goes to fund the government.

On the other hand, printing money happens behind the scenes. The government issues debt if it wants to spend, which the FED buys with printed money, thereby funding the government without you in the equation. Of course, technically, you vote for the politicians, and they vote on what to spend. Still, as we saw, the federal politicians are barely accountable to the people they represent. It is doubtful they even know what they are voting for under these 1000 page spending bills.

If taxation is the preferable method of funding the government, let's first define direct and indirect taxes. An indirect tax is something like a sales tax. You do not directly pay a sales tax to the government. Instead, you pay the merchant, who then pays the government. This allows the merchant to just add on the sales tax to whatever he is selling. The merchant says: "The government is taxing me for this sale by this much. If you want this product, you need to pay the tax." In this type of transaction, the consumer chooses to accept or reject the offer. For this reason, it is the lesser of the two evils.

A direct tax is when the government directly taxes an individual. It says: "You. Give me this much money now." A direct tax is very contradictory to the foundational principles of the United States, which is why, prior to 1913, there was no direct federal income tax unless the tax burden fell equally amongst all states.

From Article 1 Section 2:

> *"Representatives and direct Taxes shall be apportioned among the several States which may be included within this Union."*

Also from Article 1 Section 9:

> *"No Capitation, or other direct, Tax shall be laid, unless in Proportion to the Census or enumeration herein before directed to be taken."*

Direct taxes are only allowed if they are apportioned, meaning that the tax is proportionally divided amongst the states based on their population. In other words, each state pays a fair amount. The reason this makes sense is because, as James Madison said, "the power of taxation will, for the most part, be connected" to issues that concern the entire United States, like "external objects, as war, peace, negotiation, and foreign commerce." In the end, that is what the federal government is there for. Since all states are affected by these issues equally, they must each pay an amount proportional to their population. Keep in mind that these taxes would not be so high since the federal government only has a few powers anyways.

Still, why can't the federal government impose something like a sales tax. At least the sales tax is, in a sense, voluntary. Direct taxes are practically theft. Well, the federal government can only be involved in interstate commerce. It would not have the ability to tax transactions within a state. And the constitution says that "No Tax or Duty shall be laid on Articles exported from any State," so an interstate sales tax is also out of the question. A direct tax is the only option that remains.

The government does need to tax occasionally to deal with the collective problems of the United States. That is a fact that must be accepted to form this alliance of states. All states must make such a compromise to form a union. However, we mitigate the situation by limiting the federal government to necessary things like common defense.

The states must now decide how to collect the tax burden that fell onto them. They are free to choose how to do this. They can implement a sales tax within their states if they would like. Maybe they will implement a flat income tax for all citizens or a higher tax for wealthier citizens. Maybe they will get creative and only apply a sales tax on luxury items. It's their choice. The hope is that since the states are constantly in competition with one another, they cannot tax unfairly. In other words, each state will try to tax its residents in the fairest way possible so that they do indeed remain residents. Obviously, this is not true for the federal government. We have no choice when it comes to the federal government, which is again why its size and abilities should be limited.

What comes next in the taxation history of the United States is the Sixteenth Amendment:

> *"The Congress shall have power to lay and collect taxes on incomes, from whatever source derived, without apportionment among the several States, and without regard to any census or enumeration."*

This amendment alone gives way to fiat money and abusive taxation of the individual, both of which we desperately tried to avoid. It led to the formation of the IRS in 1913, which is the tax agency of the U.S. Recall that a $100 bill does not have any intrinsic value outside of its potential to be used as paper. An alien would value a $100 bill no differently than actual paper. The same cannot be said about gold. Gold has universal value because an alien would use it as a commodity, just like we do. However, if you now tell the alien that armed men will show up at his door if he does not bring back some of these $100 bills at the end of the year, they will suddenly have value to him. In other words, he will do "work" for someone who is in possession of these papers. Interestingly, 1913 also happens to be the date the Federal Reserve was established, after a secret meeting on Jekyll Island with the top banking executives of the time. It is an eerie coincidence considering that fiat money has value because you must pay taxes with it.

Funding Our Society's Government

Let's incorporate what we learned into our society. We can copy the original Constitution without the sixteenth amendment, with some minor additions.

All governments, in general, should spend the least amount of money possible. This is especially true for the federal government. With the earlier principles, we can say that lawmaking, law enforcement, and taxation should always occur at the lowest government level.

Since we do not want the federal government to be involved in commerce, we must resort to a direct federal tax rather than a federal sales tax. However, this federal tax is not on individuals. It is on states in proportion to their population, which makes sense since the federal government's powers would only allow it to take action on a matter that would concern all states. It is then up to the states to collect this tax.

States will tax their residents to collect the funds that must be sent to the federal government and also fund the operations within their state. We will deviate from the U.S. and impose an additional rule on the states. The states are not allowed to use direct taxes for two reasons. First, the competition among the fifty states may not be sufficient to deter aggressive taxation. Also, a person should not be forced to flee a state to escape aggressive taxation. Second, if a state cannot fund its operations with just indirect taxes, it is an indication that it is doing too much.

CHAPTER 9

The Pinnacle

Developing The Vision

We have reached the end. We created a society from scratch by reasoning out everything from previously established truths. The central axiom we built upon was self-ownership. This, we said, was a self-evident statement. It all gave rise to the three pillars of our society, which are sound money, free markets, and limited government. The previous chapters served to answer why we should adopt these principles. In this chapter, we should see what the global society would be like if everyone in the world embraced these established principles.

We will see that global adaptation is, in fact, the next evolutionary stage for humankind. To see this, we need to go back. So much into the past that the direction of progress becomes clear. We must zoom out enough so that the short-term fluctuations die out and the long-term trend becomes crystal clear.

Past, Present, And Future Of Humanity

Let's go back to the old days of Earth. Inside the Earth's ocean, there are some atoms. They are just floating around in the water doing nothing. Most atoms like to hang out in groups. Maybe at first in groups of 5 atoms, then 10, then 100. Some of these atomic chunks are special, though. Some chunks can make copies of themselves. They are self-replicating chunks. Chunks of atoms are called molecules. So we have these self-replicating molecules that make more of themselves. And since they make more of themselves, some amount of time later, there are a bunch of them. But not all self-replicating molecules are equally good at replicating themselves. The better replicators, over time, dominate the system because, well, they are better at replicating themselves. So although what is happening is that the better replicators just dominate the system, it seems like the molecules are actively "trying" to become better self-replicators. Over time, the number of better self-replicators increases, and the number of worse ones decreases.

How do self-replicators improve, though? Sometimes, during replication, a mistake is made. Most of the time, this leads to the improperly replicated copy being worse at self-replication, and it consequently cannot make more of itself. However, sometimes the error is beneficial, and the improperly replicated copy becomes a better self-replicator than the original. Over millions of years, the self-replicators get more and more complex through this process. Their complexity is specific to their niche, that is, the specific environment in which they self-replicate. Since they are each complex in their *specific* ways, we call each by a different name. Each is a different *species*.

We are one of the species that live on land. What complexities have we developed over time? We have a grabber called hands. We can hold and use things that are not a part of our self-replicating complex. We hold these to make tools, which make us better equipped against dangers. You know the story here. We develop markets, money, commerce, etc. We form a society. This makes survival much easier. Life becomes less about the struggle to survive and more about other things.

What kind of other things? We start thinking about our existence, the meaning of life, and how we got here. We start asking questions. It seems like we are unique in this regard. Some animals also cooperate, like wolves that hunt in packs, but it seems like they do not ask each other questions. As humans, we were struck by something at some point that made us inquisitive. Maybe God, maybe not. That is for each individual to *question* and find out for themself. But we are different. We want to know more. Perhaps other animals are also curious, but they cannot afford to explore answers as we can.

A gazelle cannot sit all day and think about its existence. It must constantly be on the lookout.

Since survival is so easy for a human, he has time to investigate questions. He ponders one day: How did I get here? One day I woke up, and I was alive. Who put me here? Why is there a big yellow ball that appears in the sky every day? Is that who put me here? It would make sense. I'm happy and warm when it shows up in the morning, and my eyes get tired when it's gone at night. Then I fall into a trance for a long time until the yellow ball automatically revives me from the trance. This yellow ball is a big deal! Let me start analyzing this thing further. How long is it in the sky every day? Interesting, not the same amount. Let me chart its trajectory across the sky. What about other things in the sky? When it's dark, I see a bunch of dots. These dots make exciting figures. The sky is so crazy! Let me share what I found with others.

Ever since then, we have been trying to figure out how the sky works. We have since come a long way. It was just the 17th century when Gallileo said that the Earth was orbiting the Sun and not the other way around. The same thing can be said about our medical science. Penicillin was found in the 20th century. We didn't have much against bacteria until then. Similarly, when it comes to anesthetics. Not long ago, the cure for an infected leg would be amputation, with a bottle of whiskey for the pain. Now you take a pill, and it's gone.

Humans have made incredible advancements, and most of these advancements were in the past few hundred years. Our development is exponential; that is, not only are we developing, but the rate at which we are developing is increasing. But why? Why isn't it increasing linearly, that is, still moving up but at a steady rate like a car going up a hill.

The answer might be the "thought network" we form as a society. We don't just have thoughts in our own heads. We share them with others, write them down, and pass them on to further generations. We believe that one thought that arose in one brain might be of use to the other brains of our society. We share that thought with others. We do so because maybe a useful piece of information will make it to someone who needs it to answer a critical question he had. He can then share his question along with his answer with the rest of us, pushing humanity one step ahead. This is a critical leap in evolution. What we are forming with our thoughts is akin to what the basic forms of life did. At some point, they went from single-celled organisms to multicellular organisms. What humans are trying to form is a multi-brained structure. One thought that is conjured in a brain is shared with another brain. We are forming a network of brains that pass thoughts amongst each other. Just like how the individual neurons inside our brains seamlessly interact with one another, the individual brains of society must seamlessly interact with one another. **It will be the next stage of human evolution.** We will form **a greater societal brain** that has information flowing seamlessly between the individual brains, which are just the neurons of the greater societal brain.

When the individual brains communicate using verbal language, the information flow is weak. It is still useful and has helped humans come a long way, but it is suboptimal due to the archaic technology it uses. Consider the journey of a thought from one brain to another brain. First, the thought conjurer projects the thought onto a set of words; that is, he assembles a string of words from his personal dictionary that best represents his thought. During this process, he loses some precision because words cannot perfectly describe thoughts. The first brain intends to send the word string to the other brain via air pressure waves. To do so, it pushes air out from the lungs and dangles a piece of meat called the tongue to make different combinations of pressure waves. The other brain hears these thanks to a pressure wave sensor called the ear and decodes them into words. Finally, the receiver takes the words and tries to recover the original thought that the sender intended. While doing so, the receiver converts from the set of words to the set of thoughts. If the thought is not spoken out loud like this, it is written. The thought must ultimately go through two [thought]<->[words] conversions, losing precision each time.

Although we do not have a better way to communicate the abstract ideas we have, other than maybe writing, pictures, or video, we do have a near-perfect way to communicate our thoughts about resource allocation. The economic part of the greater societal brain is already strongly formed; resource allocation questions and answers can be communicated fluidly amongst all the brains. Remember, the issue that plagued a society was the fact that human wants are endless, but the resources are limited. This meant that an economy had to answer three questions. What to produce? How to produce? For whom to produce? The brains that form the greater societal brain already have a way to pass one piece of economic information from one node to another in a precise manner, without having to decipher into words, not limited by language or distance, and at near-instant speeds. How so?

The neurons answering the economic questions in the greater societal brain communicate with **money.** Money is the universal language. No matter what culture, country, or language we are a part of, increasing prices mean that the greater societal brain wants more of that thing to be made or less of it consumed. It discourages consumers from using that "thing" and encourages producers to make more of that "thing." This is how we quickly figure out what to produce.

Now, it is time to figure out how to produce. Shall I make chairs out of silver? No, they will be too expensive. What does that mean? It means we don't have much of this resource called "silver," and we need it more in other parts of the globe for other things that we produce. Use something else. What about wood? Wood is great; we have plenty of it, which means it's cheap. The fact that it is cheap is the Decentralized Global Societal Brain telling me that there is an abundance of wood. All the other brains in society tell me how to produce a chair through the **market,** and they convey this information using money. If I find a way to make a chair from an even cheaper material, I undercut the other producers and collect some **profit.** Or, I might try to use wood still but find a way to assemble it in a smaller factory, saving me costs. I can then again sell the chair for cheaper and collect a profit. What does this profit indicate? The fact that I have liberated a valuable resource in the production of this chair. The Decentralized Global Societal Brain rewards me for using less land when making a chair. I get rewarded if I can make the same product using less of the limited resources. No single person tells me to do anything. The collective mind of the entire society passes the aggregated knowledge onto me and, in fact, later uses me as a local delegate to actually execute an action based on the knowledge.

The Decentralized Global Societal Brain also tells me via profit what resources to combine. I hear that graphite plus wood plus labor to make a pencil is good because the pencil sells more for what the graphite, wood, and labor costs. The Decentralized Global Societal Brain says that these three limited resources combined are better than not combined. I hear that graphite plus gold plus labor to make a pencil is bad because I calculate my cost and see that it is higher than what a pencil sells for. Selling such pencils wouldn't be profitable. The Decentralized Global Societal Brain tells me that these three limited resources are better when uncombined. Profit rewards me for making beneficial combinations of resources.

And finally, we must figure out for whom to produce. We again use the pot analogy for this. Anyone who produces something and puts it in the pot gets to pull out of the pot something of equal value. Money is again what enables this. All the brains know that if someone has money, they have, at some point, put something into the pot. We don't need to know exactly what. Money tells us instantly the value of the thing he put in, and he will now pull something out. Maybe he added something in when he lived in Japan but is now pulling out in Mexico. The Mexicans do not call up a Japanese and verify how much of what this person added. The brains instantly communicate. All of this is, of course, contingent on the fact that the money is sound.

Once again, the whole game is how to make the most out of our limited resources. If we are to produce more of something, we need to produce less of something else. If the markets are free and money is sound, the nodes instantly communicate and figure out what to make more of, how to combine resources when making those things so that scarce resources are efficiently used, and who can consume what is made from the resources.

Now finally, let's see a physical analogy for this abstract concept of the Decentralized Global Societal Brain. Imagine for a second that the two opposite sides of the world are working on the same problem, and they are connected with a string. Resources are limited, so the two groups need to share them. When one team has a really good idea, they tug the string to indicate that they have a great idea and want a bit more resources from the other side to be able to implement their solution. Money works exactly like this. We are all connected, not with strings, but with the universal understanding of money. When a company has found a great way to solve a problem, they want to increase their use of resources to implement their solution. So they demand more resources, and the price goes up. This is like tugging the string and telling all others in the network that one of us knows a really productive use for this resource. All businesses who cannot justify the new high cost of this resource understand that there is someone out there who knows how to use it better and that they should let them have it. The priced-out business can now focus on a new problem.

All of this happens without a single word. The participants can speak Chinese, English, or Arabic individually, but they all speak money.

But notice again that this only works if the money is sound and the markets are free. When governments inject money into the system, it's like they introduce slack into the strings. Communication breaks. As some nodes pull on the rope, others don't feel this request because of the slack. When they subsidize a company over another, they use their powerful hands to help a company pull the string stronger. Introducing slack into the string and helping certain companies pull the string harder is not beneficial to society. The string conveys information. True information. The Decentralized Global Societal Brain tells this company to let go of the scarce resources it's using. Society cannot use the scarce resources gobbled up by the inefficient company.

When Company A solves a problem better than Company B and drives Company B out of business, the best scenario is for Company B to take the hint that Company A should specialize in this task. Company B should find something they would be better at solving. Instead, suppose Company B is politically connected. In that case, the government offers them a bailout, subsidizes them, or puts tariffs in place that affect Company A. Politicians know how to phrase these things so that it seems like they're helping society at large, for example, by saying that millions of jobs will be preserved, tax revenue will go up, we will keep our share in the global market, etc. In reality, Company B, its lobbyists, and politicians are the only beneficiaries of this policy. The rest of the planet does not enjoy the benefit of having the more efficient Company A create this good or service. Efficiency means lower prices for consumers. So the government policy leaves consumers with higher prices and a more inefficient company. Effectively every citizen pays a bit of money to keep Company B alive.

Almost all interventions of the government in markets are like this. They disrupt the communication enabled by money, making the world less efficient at solving its problems. The signals of the market have a purpose, and disrupting them is globally harmful. Sound money, free markets, and limited government help us ensure that we are communicating effectively as nodes of a global network to maximize our potential.

What society must perform is no easy task. It must allocate resources in the most efficient way possible. The right things need to go to the right places and be combined in the right ways to produce the right products in the right amounts. No single person can know or manage the constantly changing preferences of consumers or the constantly changing variables in production. This is why no single person, or even a group of people, can run an economy. Systems that attempt to do this, like the USSR and North Korea, misallocate their resources so severely that people starve to death. They are so inefficient that they cannot even produce food, something that free-market economies have so much of that obesity has become a problem. Free markets work because, for this extremely difficult task of allocating resources efficiently, they employ all the people in the economy. No central leader knows all the relevant information, but the individual people know relevant information in their vicinities. Knowing this information, they make local decisions, and with the help of sound money, this information is communicated across the globe to everyone, regardless of what language they speak. The greater societal brain relies on 7 billion **decentralized** nodes that individually compute how resources should be allocated. It combines the power of all humans.

So then, we should explicitly mention that the greater societal brain must be decentralized. If we can do this, we will allocate our resources in the most efficient way possible, which will lead to tremendous prosperity. We will be acting like one unit, making rapid decisions on which resources must go where, be combined how, and to produce what. Our lifespans will extend. Our quality of life will be pristine. Our technology will experience huge leaps. So much that one day, we may link with another civilization that lives on another planet. And then another. We will exchange technology, information, and also products with these civilizations. We will trade our goods and services for their goods and services. Our decentralized greater societal brain will link up with their decentralized greater societal brain and form the neurons for an even greater brain. And later, that brain will become the neuron of an even greater brain. The complex structure that we will all form will be the **Decentralized Universal Brain.**

Our way to prosperity calls for three things:

Sound Money: Stop disrupting the communication.

Free Markets: Stop limiting the ability of nodes to interact with each other.

Limited Government: Stop trying to solve the problems centrally and let the nodes figure it out.

PART II

Achieving The Ideal
Society By Tweaking
The Closest One
We Have

Part II

We saw that the ideal society we derived from basic facts is exactly the same one described in the Declaration of Independence of America. Therefore, perhaps the best course of action to achieve this society would be to fix America first so that it returns to the ideals it was founded on. America is where we have the greatest head start in the liberty race and the most solid foundation we can build upon. After that, we will protect it so that it remains a strong beacon of liberty in the world. Eventually, all countries, with the help of America, will also base their foundations on liberty, sound money, and limited government.

This, however, should not be interpreted to mean that America will invade other countries. For countries that voluntarily seek help and wish to join the liberty alliance, help in non-aggressive forms can be provided by America. Examples of such help could be providing internet access to countries with oppressive governments that cut their people's communication channels, enabling people to use sound money in places where the government still abuses fiat money, allowing people who live in unfree markets to partake in the American economy through remote channels, etc. There are many ways to help other countries be freer without funding terror. Of course, there is also the American side of the voluntary equation. Americans must voluntarily choose to provide help. Of course, Americans would benefit from liberating people from tyranny since everyone, including Americans, benefit from more freedom in the world. This again follows from the reasoning that freedom leads to prosperity, and prosperity benefits all.

Part 2 of the book is dedicated to fixing the United States, although, since many other countries in the world experience identical problems, the solutions will be applicable worldwide. We will walk through the contemporary socio-economic issues, understand the reasons behind the problems, understand why the current solutions do not work, and we will propose the right solutions instead.

CHAPTER 10

Dealing with Corporations

Taxing Corporations is Deceptive

What is a corporation to begin with? A corporation is nothing but an abstract entity that encompasses the shareholders of the company. It just makes it easier for shareholders to make payments to suppliers, employees, etc., take payments from customers, and later split the financial gains or losses amongst the shareholders. It's just a device that makes finances easier for a group of people.

What are the existing taxes on a corporation? For a corporation to make a profit, it must first sell something. That something will be sold with a sales tax of 7% or so, depending on the state. Even from the onset, the money entering a corporation is taxed. Then that money makes its way to the people who are part of the corporation in one of two ways. First, employee salaries are paid. A payroll tax of 15.3% is taken from this. After handling payroll taxes, the individual pays a federal personal income tax on the remainder, ranging from 10-37%. Then he must pay a state personal income tax as well, ranging from 0-13%. So as the money makes its way to the employee, it is taxed four different times, except for the few residents of states with no income tax, who are only taxed three times.

Once all employees and other costs are paid, the profit of the corporation is calculated. The corporation pays a 21% federal tax on this profit, which was only recently reduced from previously higher rates in 2018. Then, a state corporate tax must be paid as well, ranging from 0-11.5%. Finally, when the profits are passed on to the shareholders, they pay federal and state income taxes on the distributions. That is the second way in which people are paid. So you can be assured that the money that enters a corporation does not leave without being taxed.

The first misconception this should address is the belief that corporations pay no taxes. Depending on where one resides and whether they are a shareholder or employee, they will pay four or five different taxes on the same dollar. The one trick that corporations can pull off to mitigate their tax burden is to set up a foreign company. Then they can make it look as though they do not make a profit in the U.S. and, therefore not subject to corporate taxes. However, they still are subject to payroll, sales, federal personal income, and state personal income taxes. There is no way to avoid paying these.

The second misconception we must address is the belief that raising corporate taxes would benefit the poor while hurting the rich. First off, raising the corporate tax rate would not affect the companies that evade it using foreign companies since the trick they use is to have zero profit in the U.S. anyway. It doesn't matter how high the rate is; any percentage of zero is zero. However, it will affect the corporations who are set up in the U.S. and are paying corporate taxes, though likely not in the way that you hope.

Imagine you sell apples for $1 each. Your costs add up to 90 cents, and so you profit 10 cents from each sale. Now suppose the government puts a 10% tax on apple sales. This means you must pay 10 cents for each sale of an apple, but that's how much you profited anyways. Clearly, you will not sell the apple for $1 anymore because you would not be making any money. So you raise the price of an apple to $1.10, and the consumer ultimately pays the tax. This example uses sales taxes because it is easier to understand, but the idea is the same with corporate taxes. Again let's say the apple costs 90 cents and is sold for a profit of 10 cents. This time the government taxes your profit at a rate of 50%. Since you have to pay a tax on your earnings now, you raise the price to $1.10, yielding you a profit of 20 cents, minus 50%, equal to 10 cents once again.

One objection would be that the corporation will not be able to raise prices that much; therefore, it will also have to bear the tax burden slightly. It is a valid objection; however, it still does not justify corporate taxes. A decrease in the net corporate profits due to the tax affects the shareholders. They receive less money because the corporation has to pay some tax. However, if the goal was to tax the shareholders, the government could have just increased capital gains taxes. Or, assuming the goal is to tax the rich, the government could just increase the top income tax rate. The point is that the money leaving a corporation is already taxed. Those existing taxes can be adjusted if the goal is to tax a particular group of people without passing on the tax burden to the consumers. Which brings about the question: "Why bother with a corporate tax at all?"

Exactly. The correct corporate tax rate is zero. Taxing corporations is just a trick. It is easy to convince the public of these taxes because every citizen feels like the tax will only affect the evil corporations and not themselves. Ultimately, all taxes are paid by the people. The government is reluctant to adjust the existing methods of taxation because then the people would clearly see whom the rising taxes affect. Corporate taxation is just another deceptive practice to persuade the public to a tax hike. In the end, the result is a transfer of wealth from the public to the hands of the government. The losers are the people, and the winners are the politicians and their cronies.

Subsidies Distort True Desires

The government claims that it must subsidize some industries because they would not be created if left to the free market. Or, it must subsidize certain products to reduce the cost because these items are necessities. Let's go over these claims.

To start off, understand that a free market is a voting machine. People vote with their money and essentially say, "I want/need this thing." People can have different degrees of wanting things. The more you want something, the more money you are willing to give up for it. Essentially they gather up and offer a bounty on a problem. This signals to entrepreneurs that some people would like this problem to be solved. The bounty encourages them, and they create what you want if they can. Notice how awesome this is; *your simple act of wanting something creates signals in the market that actually brings it into existence.*

This, however, is not the complete picture because everyone wants something, but we have limited resources. We cannot satisfy everyone's desires simultaneously because we don't have infinite resources. This means we have to choose which problems to solve first. Naturally, entrepreneurs decide to solve the most profitable problems first.

The reason this makes sense goes back to what profit represents. An entrepreneur profits if he is able to combine resources in such a way that consumers pay more for the resultant product than what went into it. Profit represents the excess value that is created from assembling a certain set of resources. *The most profitable problems have the largest gap between what is taken from the pool of resources and what is delivered to consumers in the end.* The most amount of value, therefore happiness, can be created if they are solved first.

So what happens with subsidies? When the government subsidizes an industry, they are essentially increasing the bounty on the problem, so entrepreneurs are more incentivized to solve it.

Imagine if, under no government intervention, problem A is more profitable than problem B. This is the case because more people will be happy if problem A is solved. We know this because everyone in the market voted with their happiness tokens, a.k.a. money, and said they preferred A over B. Now, if the government makes problem B more profitable by subsidizing it, the market would deviate from its happiness-maximizing strategy.

It is worse if you remember that the government does not have its own money. It taxes people and spends the money on their behalf. So in this situation, the government essentially voted on problem B on behalf of everyone they taxed. The fact of the matter is that if an industry cannot exist without subsidization, it is because the people prefer to devote resources elsewhere. The public is saying that they would be happier if other products were created. When left to their personal choices, the people prefer that more resources be devoted to problem A than problem B. The losers in this scenario are the people, and the winners are those who work in a company dealing with problem B. It would not be surprising if those exact companies lobbied or funded a politician's campaign.

* * *

Again, the deeper issue is how the government is great at selling these ideas that ultimately hurt the people. It's not easy to see the better choice when the government proposes subsidies. The better choice is to leave the market alone, but let's go through an example to see. Imagine a very cool, high-tech device: shoes that massage your feet. Would it be nice to have these shoes? Of course. Everyone would rather have shoes with massaging capabilities than not. So if the government subsidizes this cool product so that it gets created, would it be good for society?

It's hard to see why it is a problem to subsidize this product. Everyone now gets to enjoy this luxury. This product used to not exist, and now it does. How can that be bad? This is the classic trick of the government. They always mention what you get and never what you lose. By subsidizing this product, the government increased the product's priority in the market. So yes, we got cool shoes that massage our feet, but we also didn't get things we would've actually preferred. If left alone, we would've voted with our money to solve other problems and get those solutions first. But the government took some of our voting tokens via taxation and voted via subsidization on our behalf for a product we would not have prioritized. We each are on earth for a limited time. Before we die, we will only see a limited number of technological leaps and innovations. We ought to be able to vote on which ones.

Free Trade Benefits All

Tariffs are taxes on imported goods and services. There are two main effects of tariffs. First, the government has more money to spend since it is a form of tax. Second, it protects local industries since tariffs only apply to foreign goods and services. But, as always, we will see that these are not so beneficial and instead benefit only some people at the expense of others.

Regarding the increased tax budget, the government will say that this will lead to the funding of more government programs that help the people. However, exactly how did tariffs increase the tax budget? Well, when a foreign good is sold for $12 instead of $10 because of a $2 tariff on imports, the consumer of this product is the one who pays $2 more. So the result is a transfer of money from the people to the government, which the government will later claim is a good thing because the $2 collected can be spent on public programs. The public again fails to realize what the government takes from them while focusing on what it gives. Yes, the tax pool is filled up, but the consumers filled it up. The consumer had the $2 in his pocket before paying the tariff; that is how the tax pool filled up. Since it is more efficient for people to spend their own money on what they want, rather than have it go through layers of government bureaucracy, only to have the remaining crumbs wastefully spent on some public program that the individual did not really want, we can say the tariff is a net negative.

It is actually true that a tariff protects the local industry, but it is again at the expense of the consumers. Only the protected industry benefits, so don't be surprised if they are close friends with the government. Essentially what the consumers could buy for $10 from a foreigner, they now buy from a local for $12. Consumers pay extra to protect the local industry.

Take the example of the State of Texas and the State of Idaho. Texas has a lot of oil and, therefore, a strong oil industry. Idaho has a favorable climate for potatoes and, consequently, a strong potato industry. What if Texas suddenly said they would have tariffs on Idaho's potatoes because the Texas potato industry could not compete with the cheaper Idaho potatoes? As a retaliation, what if Idaho decided to support the Idaho oil industry by having tariffs on Texas' oil?

This is a worse situation for both Texas and Idaho. Remember the basics we derived when discussing the emergence of markets. It is beneficial for all parties to focus on what they are good at and then trade. To be clear, it would be worse even if only one state applied a tariff. The issue does not arise from retaliation. All consumers benefit from lower prices when those who are better at a job focus on that job. This is the reason we have markets in the first place. The reason a foreign product is cheaper is an indication that a foreigner can consume fewer resources when making that product. They are more efficient, so it would be better for the global society to buy from them. By enacting a tariff, we reward inefficient industries.

The borders do not make a difference. We are all just people in a global marketplace. Some places are more efficient at producing certain things than others. States do not engage in trade wars, and neither do counties, even though they also have borders. Therefore, countries should not worry about importing certain goods from other countries rather than producing them themselves. Such is the case because that country happens to be more efficient.

To illustrate the point further, we can change where the borders are drawn and start analyzing families. Your family is like a small country with a nice little economy. You and your parents each have jobs. Let's say your dad is a shoemaker, your mom knits sweaters, and you grow roses and sell them. Roses, sweaters, and shoes are your exports. You guys take the money from these exports and import your needs like food, medicine, etc. Should your family put up tariffs on food and medicine to encourage the production of these items locally within your family unit? Shortly you would notice that these items either become very expensive or are not produced at all. There is no difference between individuals trading, family units trading, counties trading, states trading, or countries trading. More trading is always better.

If our local industry cannot produce certain goods or services cheaper than foreigners, we should let foreigners produce those and focus on what we can produce for cheaper. This makes for a more efficient global society, meaning more is made from limited resources in aggregate.

Pollution

If you recall, while building our society from the ground up, we justified government intervention under only one pretense: when the NAP was violated. Pollution of the oceans, rivers, air, or all evil things that corporations typically do violate the NAP, including CO_2 emissions. Society collectively owns nature. It is our property. When a corporation pollutes the environment, it commits an act of aggression against our property, thus justifying government intervention.

They get away with it is because it is hard to defend our collective property. Imagine if a corporation dumped their trash on your front lawn. They would never even attempt this because you will take them to court right away, which is much easier than collectively suing a corporation. Additionally, one would need permission to enter your private property, whereas a corporation, for example, can pollute the ocean without first asking anyone for permission to enter.

One thought would be to regulate the industry. We should be reluctant to do this because regulation will instantly isolate the industry from new competition. With time, this will turn the industry into a monopoly and lead to more undesirable behavior. Competition is the greatest deterrent to abusive corporations. Second, the public will not know what hides in the thousands of pages of new laws. If history repeats itself, we can be sure that corporations will lobby and sponsor the bills that will regulate them. The ineffectiveness of regulation should be evident in the fact that the industries that pollute are already heavily regulated.

A better solution would be to use the market. Essentially, if we take air pollution as an example, the corporation and you participate in an involuntary exchange in which you trade your [clean air] for [dirty air]. A partial solution would be to tax the corporation and directly give you the money from the tax. This way, at least you are compensated for your exchange. Notice, though, that you must be directly compensated. The money should not remain with the government to be spent on projects without your consent. Either way, this solution is problematic for a few reasons.

First, giving you money after the involuntary exchange does not make it voluntary. Perhaps you did not want to trade your clean air at all, no matter the price. Second, it requires a governing body to determine how much the tax should be. This puts the power into the hand of the governments, paving the way for more lobbying to keep this tax low. The analogy for this situation is a man walking down the street and paying a fine for every piece of trash he litters. As a result, the man is less likely to litter, but the street still remains dirty. The people are not necessarily happy with the compensation they receive for the dirty streets. Especially not if the littering man can bribe the official giving him the fine.

We can improve this situation by forcing the man to pick up the trash. He will likely not want to do so himself, but then he must employ a person to do so. The man can throw out anything he wants, as long as he, for example, pays a person to follow him 24/7 and pick up everything he throws on the ground. This way, streets still remain clean, and the rest of society is not affected. How does this apply to corporations? If, let's say a corporation releases one ton of CO_2, it must pay another corporation to capture one ton of CO_2. The clean-up corporation could be one that specializes in this task, like one that operates carbon-capture machines or simply plants trees. Or it could be an ordinary business that captures carbon as a natural consequence of its business operations—for example, a regular farm. The benefit of this solution is that the involuntary exchange is reverted, and it is relatively simple to implement. We must create a marketplace to trade CO_2 credits, or credits for plastic, smog, etc., and ensure that corporations buy credits that undo their pollution. The problem of determining the exact amount of tax that a corporation would have to pay if the previous solution were implemented is also solved. The price per pollutant is determined by the market, which is the voice of society.

There great benefit of using a market solution is the ease of implementing policies. For example, to undo past damage, we can mandate that corporations bring in more CO_2 credits than they emit for the next ten years. We could clean the oceans by just buying ocean trash from the market. Organizations that rely on donations will have a way to fund their operations. Most importantly, though, we incorporate previously unaccounted resources like clean air, clean oceans, etc., into our economic machine that efficiently allocates resources globally. The crux of the issue with pollution is that the free market sees the polluted resources as free; therefore, it does not see a problem with using them up. All there is to do is to add a price to it.

Regulation Makes Monopolies

Regulation Benefits The Big Players

Should corporations be regulated? Aren't they extorting their customers? Aren't some corporations too big? The answer is that some regulations may be needed on occasion, but most regulations are harmful and often achieve the opposite effect.

Most people view their local businesses favorably. They even go out of their way sometimes to support them. For example, during the COVID-19 Pandemic, many people made extra effort to buy from their local stores and not some giant corporation. So when exactly does a business go from deserving love and support to deserving hate and punishments? After how many franchise stores would you start hating your local coffee shop? Or would you? If one of your local businesses expanded to the continent and grew successfully, would you begin despising them?

It wouldn't make sense to hate on them just on the basis of how much money they bring in, so most people must think that corporations are evil for some other reason. The major issues are their impact on the environment, how they aren't held to the same standards as regular businesses, how they get bailouts with taxpayer money, how they kill small businesses, etc.

On the issue of causing harm to the environment, such as pollution from factories, plastic in oceans, sewage in rivers, etc., regulations would be needed. However, the best solution would again be the market solution we discussed. The government would only need to regulate these corporations so that they indeed do pay to undo the harm that they caused. In other words, the regulation should just make sure that the amount of pollution matches the number of credits the corporation purchased.

When it comes down to the issue of corporations finding ways around laws that apply to ordinary citizens, people are absolutely right to be outraged. If there is a law, it should apply equally to all. However, it is not surprising that big corporations get an easy way out. Often companies get to a point where they start funding campaign donations or directly lobbying Congress. Would they do this if they were not getting a return on their money from a business standpoint? Of course not. That is precisely the problem. These companies are not playing fairly but instead bribing their way to the top.

When establishing why we want a free market in our society, we went over some facts from Open Secrets. We saw that the biggest lobbyers happen to be industries that ordinary citizens generally complain about, such as healthcare. These industries have the so-called "revolving door" between lobbyists and former government employees. All of this data is available for free on the non-partisan organization Open Secrets. We also noticed that the "messed-up" industries have incredibly high barriers to entry with an extensive list of regulations. We will show that these two truths are not unrelated. It is commonly thought that corporations get too big, and the government must step in and save the people from evil corporations, but in fact, it is the government that turns the corporations into monopolies by implementing regulations.

The general strategy used by corporations is to lobby the politicians, who then pass laws that either, A, benefit the corporation directly, B, hurt their existing competitors, or C, prevent the rise of new competitors. In a free market, corporations must compete with each other to offer better and better products at lower and lower prices. What you don't want is for the big players in the market to form an alliance with the government since the government has special powers given to it by the people. So the problem is not the lack of government oversight; it is the intervention in the free market.

This is a critical point that anti-free market people misunderstand. The markets in which the corporations are exploiting their customers are not free markets. Those are the markets that have a high degree of regulation, licensure, and other forms of government intervention. That is exactly what makes them "un-free." A free market welcomes competition because, well, it is free. A regulated market pushes out the competition and gives way to exploitative monopolies.

Switch back to the earlier point about pinpointing the exact moment a small company goes from deserving support to being hated. The answer may be when they start funding campaigns or lobbying. The goal of lobbying is often getting some new legislation passed. So, of course, it is not surprising if the big corporation ends up benefiting from this legislation since they essentially funded it.

Corporations have an army of lawyers that can navigate new laws as they come into action. This is why they can find ways of going around the law, which small businesses cannot do. Even if a big corporation does not find a loophole and follows the new rules exactly the same as a small business, regulation hurts the small business more. A small business cannot afford all the extra costs associated with legal fees, licenses, additional work to comply with the regulation, etc. And even if it could, it's still a high cost for a small business to bear for too long. All the extra rules don't affect the big corporations the same way it affects small businesses.

Corporations often even ask to be regulated because they know the effects regulation will have on their smaller competitors. Politicians will push to regulate an industry saying that it will benefit the public. When in reality, the big companies in that industry hired those politicians. Soon, those companies that needed to be regulated because they were "getting too big" will be massive corporations once regulations drown the smaller competitors. At that point, they will have a monopoly and will be able to exploit customers.

For example, currently, Amazon is pushing for a higher minimum wage. Amazon can afford robots, but brick and mortar stores rely on human labor, and it's often their highest cost. Raising the minimum wage affects Amazon very slightly, but it kills the small competitors. High costs of compliance with regulations eventually run small businesses out of business. Then the big corporations buy them for pennies on the dollar.

The regulation is also a high barrier of entry for new entrepreneurs that would fix the issues inside the industry, thereby lowering costs and improving quality for everyone. The regulation set out to curb a big corporation is what turns that corporation into a monopoly. The best way to prevent monopolies is to allow competition.

Competitive Industries Cannot Exploit Customers

First, you have to understand that businesses are not evil. All a business can do is offer you a good or a service, hoping that you give them your money consensually. They can never take your money. You never have to pay them a dime if the exchange they're offering you is not fair. Every time a corporation grows, it does so by offering a consumer something of value in exchange for their money. The government, via taxation, is the only entity in a free market that takes your money without you voluntarily handing it over. The government does not have to convince you with something of value in exchange for your money; you still have to pay them. Not the case with businesses.

However, the issue is when a business becomes friends with the government. Now it can use the coercive powers of the government. This exactly is what society should avoid. We don't want the referee to be friends with the players. Regulation is what enables that. It is the means by which the government reaches out into the private sector and hijacks an industry. The public is then stuck with the worst business possible: a state-endorsed monopoly.

The mistake of some people in society is to hate all businesses just because some businesses collude with the government. This then leads to them wanting more regulations. Contrary to their expectations, this empowers the big players even more.

Let's understand why fewer regulations will, in fact, be better for customers. Ask yourself: "Would you keep going to a place where you get exploited over and over again?" Just imagine a business you are not currently happy with. Why would you keep going there? The answer is that there are no alternatives. A few big exploitative monopolies run whatever industry you were thinking of. Now, why are there not any alternatives?

Remember, businesses want to have your money, but they can't take your money, so they have to convince you. If no regulations kill smaller businesses, the market has competition. As long as a business has competitors, you are the king. You decide who gets your money and who doesn't. Businesses will need to convince you somehow to hand over your money to them and not someone else, so they have no option to exploit you in the first place.

Regulation is not what prevents restaurants from poisoning their food or letting rats infest their kitchen. They want to stay in business, and any bad news will be devastating. No customer is compelled to eat at any restaurant and will leave if he feels the place is unhygienic. The customer is able to do this, though, because there is plenty of competition. Competition protects the consumer.

A great example is Airbnb or Uber. Anyone can now operate a hotel or taxi service with no license. If asked to the government, this would be extremely risky and must be regulated. What if a murderer gets on one of these platforms? What about a rapist? Will you let your child just get a ride in anyone's car? Well, first of all, how would a license prevent any criminal from committing those crimes anyways? Couldn't a murderer or a rapist get a license? The same way they got their Drivers License, perhaps. We can now see that these fear-invoking arguments from the government are exactly those; fear-invoking non-sense meant to maintain the status quo and keep existing companies in business.

Before Uber, governments had a system where if you wanted to become a taxi driver, you had to buy a special license for seriously high prices from the government, which let you operate a taxi. So the government basically owned a monopolistic taxi business—and sold the rights to become a part of that business. Some of those governments, like New York, even banned Uber when it first came out, proving that the corrupt, greedy, evil people are not running regular businesses; they are in the government running businesses. Uber and Airbnb drastically reduced the prices and benefited the everyday consumer, demonstrating how the free market benefits all.

Finally, referring to an earlier point, when the government does anything the free market could have done, you never know what you missed out on. The government would claim that there is a safe taxi network operating in the city thanks to them. But we can now see that if they had let the free market take care of this problem, we would have gotten a better and cheaper solution earlier. Imagine what other innovations we are missing out on, all the while the government claims that their solution is great. When the government taxes the people and provides a service, or in this case, prevents the market solution and instead provides its own solutions, the people always get a worse service, but they don't have anything to compare it to. So they continue to vote for the same politicians because they believe that the service would not exist without them. The fact is, if there is a need, there is a market for it, and the solution that the market comes up with is always better and cheaper. Not to mention constantly improving due to competition.

Competition ensures that the consumer stays in power. No business in a competitive industry can exploit its customers. Businesses are not malicious in the first place. They need to keep customers happy to make money. Their greed is what ensures that they treat customers properly. If a particular business is indeed malicious, the free market selects against that business as consumers naturally prefer the competitor. Therefore, if people are unhappy with a certain industry, they should not push for more competition-killing regulations in that industry.

Free Markets Already Have Regulators

Technically, a little girl's lemonade stand is a business operating in a residential area, without a license, using child labor, without collecting sales tax, probably no income tax, no health code compliance, etc. If the girl were to follow all the regulations, either her entrepreneurial spirit would be crushed, and she would never even try, or the lemonade would cost ten times more.

The example is a simple one, but it highlights the question: "To what extent are we willing to stifle the entrepreneurs who solve problems, revolutionize the world, and improve our lives?" The girl should not need to get a license that proves she can make lemonade. Nor should we need to spend an exorbitant amount of tax dollars to create an agency that regulates sugary homemade beverages and ensures that they are up to the standards set forth by the committee. The free market already takes care of this at no cost. If she cannot make proper lemonade, she goes out of business. That's the whole licensing and standards enforcing right there.

Regulations mean higher costs for business owners, translating to higher costs to the consumers and higher taxes for everyone to pay for agencies that enforce those regulations. All these extra costs come from the pockets of ordinary citizens and go towards funding the bureaucracy.

To the extent that some standardization is needed, as in if the people indeed would desire that there be some sort of guarantee that a product was appropriately made, the free market could provide this. For example, the FDA does not evaluate nutritional supplements. Reasonably, consumers might want to ensure that the pill they're about to swallow is indeed safe. You should understand by now that if there is a need for something, the free market will rise to the occasion. Like in this case, there actually are private laboratories that test each supplement and report on their findings.

Another example could be independent audit companies. These are huge private companies that audit the books of other companies. You may have heard of some of them: PWC, Ernst & Young, KPMG, and Deloitte. Their job is to audit other companies, and they compete with one another to offer this service for cheaper and better. And private businesses actually pay to be audited because it comforts their customers. If there is a need for standards enforcement, the market will take care of it. Any market solution is cheaper and better than the government's solution, which means more money is left in citizens' pockets.

Scientific journals compete in the market for reputation. There is practically no regulation that can ensure that only "the truth" is published because who can know what the truth is? Every discovery we make brings us closer and closer to knowing truly how the universe works, but we can never be certain. What we can do, though, is to report our findings truthfully. Science can be conducted in a non-corrupt way. Journals aim only to publish honest articles. Can they attract more attention by making sensational claims? Sure, and there are journals that are indeed more sensational. But this comes with the cost of being less trustworthy. Journals will have differing degrees of reputation based on their history. All the serious journals want one thing. They want to be the journal that people trust. They compete for reputation. They do this because they want to. Not because the government tells them to but because they're competing for the trust of the people. The successful ones have gained their status because people have trusted them after many years. Perhaps a journal can accept a bribe to publish misleading research, but it would quickly lose the public's trust when discovered. Competition ensures that entities act honestly.

Investigative journalism works the same way. A journalist can be corrupted but would risk losing his reputation. Universities essentially do for a person what the FDA does for a drug. They say that the subject person does indeed have the abilities he claims to have. Can universities take bribes and issue degrees? Of course. But they lose their reputation, and people grow less trusting of the future degrees they grant. All these examples illustrate how we actually can and already do have a working free market of "trust." In the next section, we will see why it is better to trust the free market regulators than the government regulators.

It's Better To Have Private Regulators Than Government Regulators

We have seen that the free market naturally creates its regulators when there is a need for them. Knowing this fact, it is clear why we do not want the government to be the regulator, licenser, standards enforcer, etc.: they have no competitors. When it comes down to it, this is the most important reason why a free market regulator is better than a government regulator.

What incentive does the government have to be honest, not take bribes, and remain impartial on cases between campaign donors and regular citizens? Nothing. The government repeatedly lies and is corrupt in the sectors in which it operates. So why does the public prefer the disreputable government over private businesses?

Why couldn't a private business do what the government does and give accreditations when needed, set standards, and control the quality of products? We saw above that there are many examples of such companies performing precisely those tasks. The public would not trust private businesses to do their job honestly, but what reason do they have to trust the government instead? When did the people in the government become saints?

People say that the private regulators would be driven by profit, which would corrupt them. It is true that people can be corrupted. But those people exist both inside the government and inside the private sector. Profit does not corrupt people; money corrupts people. The people inside the government still like money. They are the same species as the rest of us. What makes people think that the government is made up of super-human entities who would never be corrupted? The fact of the matter is that profit actually prevents corruption. The private regulators need to profit, so they need you to hand over your money to them voluntarily. They need to make sure to keep your trust. The government does not need to profit. The FDA does not need to earn and keep your trust in order to get funding next year. That is what makes an institution corruptable: when the consumers have no other option.

The great advantage of using private regulators is the ability to choose alternatives. Private regulators want to profit and remain in business, so they must keep your trust. If they don't, you do not have to keep giving money to them. When the government is corrupt, the public has no choice but to rely on the same regulators, licensers, and quality controllers. Sure, maybe the government puts the bad actors on leave, reshuffles the people in the agency, or maybe even fires some people, but in the end, it is the same organization that will continue operating again next year. In a free market, you have a choice, which means a dishonest agency automatically votes itself out by the forces of the market. This is the advantage of the market over the government. There is always a check for quality.

Let's see an example of how a conversation would play out between a doctor and his patient:

"Hello Doctor, my knee hurts a lot."

"I'm sorry to hear that. I can offer you Drug A and Drug B."

"Thank you. Have these drugs been tested for side effects and addiction potentials?"

"Yes, sir. Drug A has worked with Regulatory Agency X, and Drug B has worked with Regulatory Agency Y."

"Ooh. Wasn't Regulatory Agency Y involved in that addiction scandal with the opioid drugs?"

"Yes, sir. Perhaps you would like to go with Drug A then?"

"Yes, I believe that would be the wiser choice."

The lesson is that private businesses can be corrupt, true, but so can the government. However, the thing about a private business is that no one forces you to do business with them the next year. After a corruption scandal, they lose their customers. You take your business to a trustworthy company.

No Corporate Bailouts

The reason we support the free market is that it is fair. The market does not care if a product is produced by a black worker or a white worker, male or female, gay or straight. It only cares about efficiency. It only answers the question: "How can we use the limited resources we have as a society and deliver a better and cheaper product?" It rewards merit and only merit.

A fair society should be just like this. It should have only one metric, which is "success," because when one of our citizens succeeds, we all benefit. Sure, the successful person benefits the most, but so does everyone else by virtue of lower prices and better quality items—since the only way you can succeed in a free market is by offering more quality for less. This mechanism of the free market should never be broken. One should only succeed if he has provided something better for cheaper.

Our stance is always against the disruption of this free market mechanism. Government demands money using the force of law, not by offering something of quality for less, then spends this money on behalf of the citizens. When it spends it on subsidies, it rigs the game in favor of a business. When it applies a tariff, it benefits a specific industry. When it enacts regulations, it creates monopolies by bankrupting smaller businesses and raising the barriers to entry for new businesses, again benefiting only the monopolies. The situations in these examples are all unfair interventions in the market. The government enriches itself and the politically connected not on the virtue of merit but by using the force of law to collect and spend money.

It is unfair to put ordinary rich people, who have earned their wealth by creating beneficial products for society, and the politically connected elite, who rely on corruption to enrich themselves, in the same category. The main difference is that the ordinary citizen who achieves wealth does so by offering quality products for cheaper, thus enriching every other citizen on his way to the top. On the other hand, a well-connected elite uses the power of the government and enriches himself at the expense of society, which is a significant difference.

A corporate bailout is another harmful government intervention that benefits the elite. It is when the government helps out a business, usually by providing some liquidity or sometimes by buying its troubled assets. The free market would dictate that as long as no rules were broken, those who succeed are entitled to their winnings, and those who lose are not compensated for their losses. Not only do politically connected corporations win unfairly by utilizing government power, but they also want compensation for their losses. Whether it be from the left-wing or right-wing, politicians are eager to form alliances with corporations. Although they claim to care about the people on the campaign trail, most are just there to help the well-connected at the expense of the very people who vote for them.

* * *

The main arguments for the bailout are that bankruptcy will leave many without a job and that society will lose a successful business. The latter point is ironic because if the company has failed, it has done so because it was not good at what it did. The market has ruled that this company was not as good as its competitors in providing a quality product. By bailing out a company of such sort, society basically approves of an inferior company.

Let's say the company is a startup with no competitors, but it failed because it could not turn a profit. That means that no one in society valued the service provided by this startup. Society spoke through the market and said, "Stop using the scarce resources; we don't want what you're making!" So by bailing out a failing company, society decreased its prosperity.

Even though, in the short term, the apparent outcome of a bankrupt company is the disappearance of the company, the long-term effects are that resources are freed up for more efficient companies to use. Until the long-term effects take hold, the choice for society seems like either having an inefficient but still somewhat productive company or nothing, which is why politicians can quickly gain support for bailouts. We again see how politicians always tell you one side of the equation. Yes, we lose the inefficient failing company, but we gain the resources locked up by the company.

Unemployment is similarly a short-term side-effect. Remember that resources are limited, and to achieve the most prosperity for the society in aggregate, we have a system in place in which every company competes with one another for scarce resources. The companies that can make the most out of the scarce resources succeed. The free market automatically allocates the resources to the most efficient businesses. These scarce resources include humans as well. That is why companies have a "Human Resources" department. Unemployment that follows a company's dissolution is a temporary freeing of scarce human resources until more efficient companies can offer those people new jobs.

Every scientist, engineer, technician, etc., is limited in quantity, and businesses compete for these individuals. The fact that a company is failing means that it was not making good use of its resources. In other words, all the raw materials, land, and also employees that belong to that company should be under a better, more efficient company. As the failing company lets go of the resources, more efficient companies pick them up. Efficiency means that more products are made from those scarce resources, meaning society is more prosperous.

If the inefficient company used tons of steel in its operations, no one would stress over the unemployment of steel if the company went under. They can understand that other companies would just buy the steel. The same is true for laid-off people. It just takes time because hiring is a time-consuming process, unlike buying steel. People who are laid off eventually find new jobs, and they can create more value for society in those new jobs since they no longer work for an inefficient company.

So far, we have seen that it is better for society if people are laid off from inefficient businesses. But you may ask: Who will employ these people who lost their jobs and how? With what money? The answer is: Exactly with the money that the government would take from us to fund the bailout. Recall that the government cannot do anything other than take one group's money and give it to another group. The money that will be offered to the failing company to pay their workers will come from the rest of society. So had the government not intervened, the rest of society would have employed the newly unemployed people using the very same dollars they handed over to the government. Once again, this is a case of the government ringing the alarm bells, taking one dollar from the rest of society, and giving that dollar to the failing business. If society had kept the dollar, they could have employed the jobless in their own businesses with that dollar.

A bailout is nothing but a game of money transfer from ordinary companies to politically connected companies in the name of averting a crisis. The connected elite earns wealth at the expense of society, and the survival of the less efficient business deprives society of prosperity.

* * *

Perhaps there is no better example of corporate bailouts than the 2008 Global Financial Crisis. The basics of the crisis are as follows. The big banks gave out bad mortgages. They made good money on these mortgages for a few years, but the bubble was brewing. They understood that these mortgages they held would fall off a cliff shortly. Banks sold the mortgage products to their unsuspecting customers and bet against the very same mortgages themselves. The bubble popped, and innocent customers lost their savings. Banks were not exactly lossless either, but the government bailed them out because they were "too big to fail."

Wall Street had a severe level of criminality: collusion, breaking fiduciary responsibilities, lying to Congress (which you can witness by watching the Congressional hearings yourself), etc. Yet the government, knowing that banks threw the time bomb at unsuspecting average Americans, chose to bail them out. Banks did not shy away from paying their top executives bonuses after bailouts either. This is not the free market in action; it is the opposite of the free market. It is "Big Government" helping its best friends at the expense of taxpayers.

If the bailouts were actually paid by direct taxation of citizens, there would be a far greater outrage than there had been. Since the government can print the money, the payment comes in the form of a subtle inflation tax or will come due as the national debt payments come due. This is why it is critical that there be sound money. It keeps the government directly accountable to the people. If money is spent, which eventually comes out of the citizens, it should be honest. Inflation and borrowing are subtle ways of hiding the costs imposed on the taxpayer.

After the crisis, the bigger banks bought the already huge banks that were in trouble. Now the banks are even bigger than they were in 2008, meaning they will again and forever be "too big to fail."

* * *

In spite of all that we have seen, there should still be lobbying. If a particular group desires to make a case to the government, they should be able to. At the very least, it is an exercise of free speech. Then, you might ask, how will the problems associated with lobbying disappear? Well, why exactly is lobbying bad? We have been saying all along that it is no problem for two people to talk and make a deal. However, the issue is when the government is one of these parties because the government has special powers over all the other members of society. That is the problem. The big corporation wants the government to rig the system in its favor. The way to prevent rigging the game is not to ban lobbying; it is to take the rigging power from the hands of the government. Take away the government's ability to intervene in commerce, as the constitution intended, and see if corporations still lobby.

Price Controls

Price controls are simply laws that dictate what the price of a good or service ought to be. The reason why they are harmful is the same reason why any other market intervention is ultimately worse for society. The free market is a communication machine. When the price of anything is high, it signals that many people want this thing, but there is not that much of it. It allows all participants to coordinate their use of resources. Those who have a good enough solution to a problem that justifies the high price of the commodity are the ones who buy it. All else must find alternative resources.

Yes, the market is not lenient and a bit cut-throat when it acts this way, but those who criticize it fail to realize that it is out of necessity, not sadistic greed. We simply have limited resources and must ration them. Failure to understand this fact leads to policies that attempt "price setting." The market price is a fact reflecting the scarcity of some good or service. One cannot just declare the price of some product and expect scarcity to no longer be an issue.

The only way to truly reduce the price of anything is to tackle the cause of the high price. That would be the scarcity. The high price is just the symptom of the issue. The true cause is too little supply for too much demand. But politicians love to put bandaids on the symptoms without fixing the causes. And That is what price ceilings are: simple attempts at fixing a supply issue with a law. The absurdity of attempting to lower prices by decree is apparent at the extreme. If such a thing is possible, let us also declare the price of mega yachts to be $1. In fact, why stop there? Let's declare the price of meat at also $1 per pound. Why don't the third-world countries just do that and eradicate poverty? What are prices anyways? Just imaginary numbers we make up. No, prices convey information about where we stand currently with our production. They tell us how much of what resources we have and how strongly people want them. We cannot just set them by law. Well, we can because we have the ability to write whatever law we want, but what we mean is that regardless of what the law says, the problem will persist economically.

Let's use lumber as an example. Suppose the market price of lumber is $10. The only way to lower the cost would be to produce more lumber or wait for there to be fewer demanders of lumber. But suppose now the government decides to mandate the price to be $5 to "make it more affordable." The fact that the price was $10 before the mandate means that there were individuals who were willing to pay $10. Now, when the price is $5, there are be even more people who would like to acquire lumber; if there were demanders at $10, there must be more demanders at $5. From the side of lumber sellers, the situation is the opposite; there were sellers willing to sell at $10, but even fewer sellers would like to sell at $5. So the reduction of price from $10 to $5, resulted in an increase in buyers and a decrease in sellers, also known as a shortage.

This means that only a lucky few will buy the lumber at $5 until it runs out. These people will be happy. But, the rest of society is unhappy. Since the market price was $10 before the ceiling, we know that there are buyers who would be happy to buy lumber even at a price higher than $5. And, we know that there are sellers that would be happy to sell to these buyers. However, the price ceiling makes the voluntary exchange between these two parties illegal. Only the lucky ones who are able to grab some lumber before it runs out are happy.

The secondary effect is more detrimental. If a price ceiling is in effect, it is likely because the people are unhappy with the high price of something. The true cure would be to increase the supply of this something. This would be what would happen in the free market because the producers would look at the price and deduce that, clearly, more of this something is needed. They do not necessarily think in the story-like manner described here, like, "Oh, the collective voice of society needs more of this resource to be produced. I must come to their help." They are just driven by profit, and the high price incentivizes them to produce more. Although, technically, the collective voice of society is asking for more production, the producer need not understand this. He can just be selfishly driven by profit and still do what society needs from him. That is, to produce more. And so he, and many other producers, do produce more until the prices go down again. The issue is solved, and the consumers unhappy with the high prices are relieved. However, if a price ceiling is in effect, more production is not incentivized, and the actual cause of the issue is never resolved.

Therefore the effect of setting prices is two-fold. First, it makes happy the few who are lucky to buy but prevents voluntary exchange from taking place amongst the rest of society, thereby making them less happy. Second, it prevents society's ability to cure the actual cause of high prices, which is scarcity, by discouraging producers from producing more.

While we are on the issue, let's explore two debated price control issues: rent control and minimum wage.

Rent Ceilings

A rent ceiling is the government's attempt at lowering rents by setting a price above which it is illegal to rent out apartments.

Exactly like the lumber example, the result of this policy is a shortage. In this case, the resource supplied is housing. This means it is challenging to find housing since there are so many potential renters but few landlords willing to rent out. Again, those who are lucky enough to find housing are satisfied, but a whole group of people unable to find housing is left unsatisfied. Again, this group would be willing to pay more to be put out of their misery, and some landlords would take them up on this offer, but it is illegal for them to match.

Rent ceilings can also give rise to unwanted side effects. A shortage of landlords and a surplus of renters place the landlords in a very powerful position. The term sometimes used is "slumlord." Since there is a long list of renters who are willing to fill the spot of any tenant who leaves, landlords do not take care of their apartments. Maintenance is often lousy, and the buildings are dirty and broken down. And, since the houses must be legally rented out for less than their market worth, the landlords accept payment in "other methods." The landlord can request the difference between the market value of the rental and the ceiling price through other means. Obviously, not all landlords do this. However, it leaves the renters vulnerable to such exploitation. Needless to say, this intervention in the market is counterproductive to its intent.

The only way to reduce rent costs would be to solve the scarcity issue, meaning more houses. The market price is high because the market speaks the reality, not because the landlords are evil people. What is the reality? There are not an infinite number of houses, and a lot of people want to live in these houses. The funny thing is that usually, the rent costs are unaffordable in cities with very tight zoning laws, building codes, lots of permitting, etc., preventing new housing development. These regulations prevent new housing from being built to address the cause of high rent: insufficient housing. Rather than relaxing these laws and solving the scarcity issue, the government doubles down and implements a rent ceiling.

Minimum Wage

Minimum wage is also a price-setting mechanism. Rather than a price ceiling, a minimum wage is a price floor because it sets a minimum. The effect is very similar, just with producers and consumers flipped. Wage is just a special name we give for the price of labor. The sellers of labor are the workers, and the buyers of labor are the businesses. When a minimum wage is set higher than the equilibrium price, there will be workers who are willing to work for less, but there will be fewer businesses that are willing to hire for the higher wage. This again leads to a shortage of job openings, or a surplus of workers, depending on what side it is looked from. Another word that describes this situation is "unemployment." So we could have zero unemployment if we let the price of labor find its equilibrium.

As in the lumber case, there would be workers willing to work for less than minimum wage and businesses that could hire them, but the law makes it illegal for them to match. Again the lucky workers find jobs, and the rest are unemployed, making zero dollars when they would have been happy to make below minimum wage. When people push for a higher minimum wage, they seem to think that the issue is synonymous with giving more money to workers. However, the truth is that some workers will earn a few dollars more, and other workers will earn a grand total of zero dollars when they are unemployed. That means that for the lucky ones, life will be better; they will earn higher wages. But for the unlucky, life will be worse for two reasons. The first is because they now earn zero dollars. The second is because wages make up a portion of the costs of goods and services. Therefore, higher wages translate to higher prices. The unlucky ones are first hit with a job loss, then with an increase in the price of products.

The objection is this: "Raising the minimum wage will not lead to unemployment because corporations are not paying their employees market prices. They are paying less than market value, so the state must use its power to demand that corporations pay a fair amount."

First of all, the fact that unemployment exists is inconsistent with the idea that workers are underpaid. Unemployment means too few jobs givers and too many job seekers. If workers could indeed be hired below the market rate, why wouldn't there be more job givers? The situation is the opposite; workers are overpaid. That is why there are not enough people willing to offer them jobs.

Second, to suggest that workers are underpaid implies that they are paid less than the value they create for the company. To see why this is not possible, let us replace the worker with a machine that prints a $10 bill every hour. The value of this machine to its owner would be $10 per hour. Suppose the seller of this machine is holding an auction to determine who will get to rent this machine. The seller opens the price at $0 per hour to rent the machine. Of course, all the greedy buyers would love to rent the device for $0 per hour and generate $10 per hour, so they all bid. The maximum anyone would bid would be $10 per hour. No one would bid even one cent higher than that. However, until that price is reached, the bidding will not stop, and the device will not be sold for less than the value it generates. What ensures that the device sells for its worth is not a law but instead bidding. In other words, competition. The same applies to workers. Businesses compete for workers. If a company underpays a worker, its competition will offer him a job at a higher wage. That will carry on until the worker gets his fair market value.

So the dynamic of a minimum wage implementation plays out like this. Say the values that two employees generate for the business are $7 and $9, and the owner pays them both $7 each. The owner pays the first worker what he is worth and underpays the second one by $2. Now, a minimum wage of $9 per hour is implemented. The underpaid worker is now properly paid, but the worker that generates $7 per hour is now costing the owner $2. Keeping him employed would be equivalent to just telling him to stay home and giving him $2 as a charity. So, he fires him. If not, he must squeeze more value out of him, meaning maybe he cuts his bathroom breaks. But, the worker will likely not want to work in those conditions, so he is fired instead. As a result, one worker loses his job, and the other receives a raise. But the thing is, in a free market, the more value-generating worker would have received a raise anyways; if the owner wouldn't increase his wage, the competitor business would eventually offer him $9. Therefore, the minimum wage is a meaningless policy that can only go on until all workers are replaced by robots.

CHAPTER 11

Indecent Goods and Services

Illegal Drugs

Besides taking us off the gold standard, Nixon is also responsible for the so-called War on Drugs. We can confidently say at this point that we have lost this war. Drugs are still around after fifty years of endless spending and enforcement. Drug epidemics have taken over certain towns, smuggling is still active, violence is prevalent, arrests and incarcerations persist, and the addiction rate is unaffected. So why does the war continue in the face of mounting evidence that it is not working?

What Are Drugs?

A drug is defined as a substance that alters the user's state of mind. Just about anything that enters your body and affects your mood can be classified as a drug, including benign substances like food and oxygen. According to the definition of a drug, food and oxygen are definitely qualified. A person who ingests food feels a mild euphoria, relaxation, stress relief, etc. The same can be said for oxygen. However, the general public would not put these substances in the same category as weed, cocaine, ecstasy, etc., although all these belong to the set of mind-altering substances. Clearly, as a society, we draw a line somewhere. We feel like there is a degree of mind-alteration we are "okay" with. Where is that line?

You may say the line is drawn at necessities. Food and oxygen are drugs that are legal because, without them, we will die. They are necessary for survival, so they must be legal. However, what about sugar. Sugar is very addictive and euphoric and not necessary for survival. How about diet coke? Most of us would agree that the line is not drawn at survival. We should acknowledge that there is an appeal to altered states of mind. Throughout their existence, humans from all around the globe have looked for different ways to explore altered states of mind. We have tried licking venomous frogs, chewing plants, extracting chemicals from cacti, crushing tree roots, and burning flowers. We did not do these to survive but instead to change our brain chemistry. So, where do we draw the line then?

Maybe the line is drawn at the point at which drugs begin hurting the user. But then, what about alcohol and cigarettes? Millions are in hospitals due to alcohol-induced harm, and alcohol is more addictive than most people think. The same is true for cigarettes. These drugs have become so ingrained in our culture that they have become normalized. Surely everyone can remember hearing someone bragging about how much they can drink. It is not uncommon to tell funny stories of binge drinking to the point of throwing up. Imagine telling a loved one about a new drug you abused so much that it made you throw up. They would likely be concerned. We have legalized harmful and addictive drugs, so the line is not at the point of causing personal harm either.

What about causing harm to others? Again, alcohol and cigarettes can be used as examples. Cigarette smoke can cause harm to those in the vicinity. Alcohol leads to the death of unrelated citizens due to drunk driving. Our existing legal drugs negatively affect non-users. However, we have passed laws to mitigate the harms that third parties experience from cigarettes and alcohol consumption. We have made it illegal to drive drunk or smoke indoors. So, it seems like society has drawn the line here. We have agreed that people are free to consume a drug but not free to affect others while doing so.

Now the question is whether this is the right line to draw? According to our principles, yes. Remember self-ownership and voluntarism. Since you own yourself, you are free to choose what to put in your body. And, you are free to buy that drug from any person that voluntarily trades with you. The caveat to voluntary exchange is the rule that the exchange should not affect anyone outside the consenting group. If others who do not consent are affected at all, government intervention is justified. In a free society, adults should be allowed to make free choices, even if it damages their health, as long as they do not harm others. The government's job is not to be our nanny; it is only to protect our rights. In that case, shouldn't more drugs be granted legality?

Some will still say no, thinking that drugs affect those other than the consumer. For example, they will claim that drugs cause neighborhoods to become epicenters for gang violence. Or, if drugs infiltrate the schools, they will negatively affect the kids. This chapter aims to show that these worries, although legitimate, would not materialize if drugs were legal. The negative connotations people ascribe to drugs should actually be directed at the drug policies. It is not drugs but rather how we deal with them that causes problems. Certainly, we are not claiming that drugs are good or healthy. They have the potential for abuse and addiction, and they can absolutely cause harm to the user. But that is not the issue. The issue is protecting non-drug users from the users.

Benefits To Society

The United States should know better how to deal with drugs because an experiment was performed a long time before the War on Drugs. It was called "Prohibition." We banned alcohol in the entire country, only to re-legalize it years later. What we experienced during the bad taught us that even if a substance is harmful, like alcohol, banning it causes more harm to society than keeping it legal. Let's see exactly how.

Have you ever heard of Al Capone, Bootlegging, or Organized Crime? They are showed us that banning a substance does not stop its usage, but it does create other problems. Think about why there was a market for alcohol in the first place. Clearly, if people did not want alcohol, there would not be a market for it. After alcohol was banned, the demand for it did not disappear, but certainly, the suppliers for it had to vanish from the open legal markets. So what happened? Well, a black market had to be created. A black market supplies those goods and services that laws make illegal to supply but which society still demands. Because, of course, as long as there is a want, there will be those who are willing to satisfy that want. Making a product illegal does not change the fact that people still want it. Only the communication of the demander and supplier is made illegal. They can no longer use the open market to communicate. They will have to communicate secretly in the black market.

A black market always causes trouble. It created problems back in the Era of Prohibition, and it creates problems with drugs now. There were gangs that sold alcohol. There was smuggling of alcohol. There were illegal productions of alcohol. Most importantly, though, there was a great deal of violence related to alcohol. The same goes for all illegal drugs right now. We see gangs, smuggling, manufacturing, and violence around illegal drugs. After the legalization of alcohol, these all ceased to exist. Why? Alcohol itself has not changed. People still enjoy alcohol, and it is still very much a part of American Culture. The reason is that alcohol is out of the black market and back in the open market now. This can serve as historical evidence, but we must also logically prove how the black market is responsible for all our drug-related troubles today.

Everything comes down to one simple thing: money. There is a demand for illegal drugs, the same way there was still a demand for alcohol after the ban. Who will fulfill this demand? Definitely not a local store, pharmacy, or supermarket, since they cannot break the law. Some regular citizen must be the one who sells drugs (or alcohol). Great, we now created a drug dealer. Where will they get their supply from, since manufacturing is also illegal? Well, either from an unlawful manufacturer or from another country with looser enforcement. You see, now we created a manufacturer. Who will bring the drugs from the foreign country? That would be the smuggler. The last piece is the protector. The state police will protect a legal business owner, like a baker, but no one will protect the drug dealers. So the dealers must assemble into a network of trusted people and protect themselves. This is what you call a gang.

Gangs fight for two reasons. The first is to enforce their rules. As we established, all enforcement comes from violence. In our peaceful society, only the threat of violence is usually enough to settle most matters. This is because the state, which is the enforcer of laws, holds a monopoly on violence. If Person A steals from Person B, the police arrive, and Person B generally returns what he stole. It makes no sense for Person B to fight with the police force, which outnumbers his violence capability. However, if Gang A steals from Gang B, the settlement may not go so smoothly. If the gangs have similar violence capabilities, they may be compelled to fight it out with their guns.

The second reason is due to territory. Since regular businesses cannot sell drugs, there is a decrease in supply. The decrease in supply leads to higher prices for the drugs, which means the gangs selling the drugs make great profits. With little competition, there is potential to form a regional monopoly on drugs. Businesses like monopolies because competition forces them to reduce prices. Gangs are essentially businesses, so they like to have monopolies as well. Since drugs are illegal, the sellers cannot just lobby the government to enact laws that would guarantee them a monopoly; they must do this themselves. This is what gang violence ultimately comes down to. The fighting is over which gang will sell to which region. Gangs protect their monopoly not with the power of the state to enact regulation but instead by using their own power.

You see, drug dealing, smuggling, illegal manufacturing, and gang violence all stem from the fact that a product is sold on the black market. These problems do not stem from drugs themselves; they stem from drugs being illegal. When alcohol was illegal, the exact same things happened. If even water is made illegal, the exact same things will happen. The specific good or service has no significance; it is the black market that causes problems.

The legalization of drugs would have two main benefits to society. First, billions will not be spent on enforcing smuggling laws, catching dealers, infiltrating gangs, doing drug busts, etc. Again think about it from a "limited resources" perspective. We do not have infinite resources, and our job as a society is to allocate these scarce resources effectively. What we free up from drug enforcement can be used to produce other goods and services.

Second, society will benefit from the disappearance of gangs, trafficking, violence, etc. It will regain all the unlivable real estate due to gang violence. Millions involved in the trafficking, manufacturing, and distribution of drugs will be able to help society in other ways. Millions who are incarcerated for non-violent drug-related offenses will be able to contribute to society. They go from costing taxpayers money in jail to working productive jobs that benefit society.

From the beginning, we said that our goal was to protect non-drug users from the users. The state's role is to protect the rights of the unconsenting parties in an exchange. We see that the harm caused to the rest of society stems from drugs being illegal. Therefore, it would be best to legalize them first. Then we can go into the more minor details like protecting against driving under the influence of drugs. We can easily solve these problems by adding a vice-tax to all drugs. This tax will go towards funding the enforcement programs. This way, the non-drug users will not even have to pay to prevent these problems, which is fair since they are not causing them.

Benefits For The Users

When drugs are legal, you may choose to do heroin. You are free to do with your adult body as you wish. No one has the right to tell you not to do so. However, most likely, you still will not do it. What prevents you from doing heroin is not its illegality. You just don't want to do it. If you abstain from a certain drug when it's illegal, you will still abstain when it's legal. However, in addition to the societal benefits outlined in the previous section, legalization has certain benefits for the users.

Now, we said our goal is to only protect non-users from the possible problems that users may cause. The state's job isn't to protect grown adults from themselves. However, it is still a positive if our legalization policy ends up benefiting the users as well. Remember, the category of drugs includes alcohol and cigarettes as well. You are likely the user of some drug. One benefit you derive from legality is quality.

Those who drank alcohol when it was legal still did so when it was illegal. They just drank a dirtier product. When alcohol was legal, the consumer enjoyed a clean, well-made product without contaminants. One unit of alcohol always got him to feel the same. During the Prohibition Era, though, what got him buzzed last week, could overdose him next week. There was no consistency in batches. And, who knows what nasty chemicals the alcohol was mixed with and what containers it contacted during smuggling. Wouldn't it be better if we could all get our uncontaminated standard-dose drugs from the pharmacy safely without bothering each other?

A worry might be kids. Let's address this. How do kids begin drugs? Maybe a dealer infiltrates a school or sells to kids on the street. But would a professional pharmacy ever sell to kids? Of course not. So then, it is better for drugs to be legal if we want to protect our kids. There are no dealers for legal substances. I'm sure no one ever tried to sell you a pineapple in a dark alley. Why? Well, because there is an open market for pineapples. There is no reason to buy from a dealer what can be bought at a market. Dealers only exist to sell illegal goods. You may argue that if the open market is not available to kids due to their age, a black market will form where adults buy drugs legally and sell them to kids. This is unfortunately true. If there is a want, a market will exist. There is likely a black market today where high schoolers buy alcohol from adults at a premium. There is nothing we can do to prevent a black market from forming. If the high schoolers want something, there will be those willing to supply it. When drugs are legal, there will be a black market where kids are sold drugs. However, that black market exists now as well. What creates that black market is not the fact that drugs have been legalized; it is the fact that high schoolers are willing to pay for drugs. In other words, currently, the entire society buys drugs from the black market. If drugs are legalized, the adult population will be able to exit the black market. Nothing changes for the kids, but the black market shrinks drastically, and society is saved from the consequences of black markets.

Cannabis

Cannabis is the first drug outside of alcohol and nicotine to be legal in some states. Federal legalization has still not been made, but it seems likely. Most Americans admit to trying cannabis or plan to try it if it gains legal status in their state. With so many citizens looking favorably at this drug, even after years of negative propaganda, one wonders why this drug was even banned in the first place and why it is still illegal.

Again, we will hear another story of a government-backed monopoly. William Randolph Hearst was a wealthy businessman living in the 1930s and the owner of a media empire. He was also heavily invested in the timber industry. The flowers of the cannabis plant are smoked as a drug, but the rest of the plant has incredibly strong fibers. These fibers are used to make what is called hemp. At the time, the paper was made from timber, but the market was ready to select hemp, given its stronger and cheaper fibers. The switch from timber to the higher quality, low price plant would benefit consumers since they would get a better product by paying less. However, it would disrupt the timber industry, in which Hearst had investments.

Hearst ran a smear campaign on cannabis using his media empire and political ties. This was how cannabis got the name "marijuana." Hearst's goal was to associate the plant with Mexicans and turn the public against it. Because Hearst had a media empire, the disinformation could be quickly spread. The plan was successful, and with the Marijuana Tax Act of 1937, Hearst ensured that his timber investments would not fail. You may attribute the success of Hearst to his media empire, thereby finding fault in capitalism. However, Heart could have published all the lies he wanted, but without the power of the government to outlaw his competition, he would not get anywhere. Regardless of his disinformation campaign, the hemp industry would have replaced timber if it wasn't for the government's regulation power. This is certain because consumers would naturally always prefer the cheaper and better product, which would be hemp.

Many industries today benefit from illegal cannabis as well. The prison industry would not enjoy liberating non-violent offenders. The pharmaceutical companies would not like this unpatentable plant stealing the market share of some of their drugs. There may even be a potential to replace some petrochemical products with hemp-derived chemicals. These businesses, of course, do not want to be disrupted by competition, but what matters is not the profit of these big industries. What matters are the benefits society would draw from consuming a cheaper and better product than what the corporations currently offer.

Although legalizing all drugs "feels" wrong to many, hopefully, we can all get behind at least legalizing cannabis federally. Some states have already taken matters into their own hands, but now we have an odd situation. In the same country that holds people in prison for tiny bits of weed in their pocket, industrial-sized operations produce tons of cannabis. It is time to free non-violent offenders from prisons and bring cannabis into the free market. That means no special licenses to grow either. We can have obvious rules like restricting sales to minors, but no strict regulation that deters competition. We do not want to form "Big Cannabis."

Other Vices

Prostitution

Whether you are morally for or against prostitution should not play into your opinions on its legality. In a free society, if two consenting adults would like to make a trade, they should be able to. You may find it wrong to hire a prostitute or become a prostitute. That is a belief that you are entitled to hold. But that just means that you should not hire a prostitute or become a prostitute. You do not get to impose your beliefs on others. The only time a citizen should complain about the exchange amongst other citizens is if there are residual effects on himself. We went over examples such as a polluting factory. The factory's operation affects the air quality of third parties who do not consume the factory's products. Therefore, they have the right to object. If the exchange between a prostitute and a customer does not affect anyone else, there is no necessity to ban it.

However, you may be thinking that prostitution does affect third parties. Again we will show that this is not true. The explanations will be very similar to those made for drugs. This is because, ultimately, the situation is the same: a good or service operating in the black market.

Recall from the drugs section that gangs form to protect themselves. Since the police do not protect their illegal business, they must take matters into their own hands by ganging up. And while the police have a monopoly on violence, the gangs can be equally matched. This means that although a threat of violence by the police is usually enough to enforce laws, gangs may need to display actual violence to protect themselves.

In the prostitution business, the parties involved are the prostitutes, customers of prostitutes commonly referred to as Johns, and the prostitutes' managers called Pimps. You may ask why the Pimp is a part of this transaction. Why can't prostitutes and Johns meet and transact alone? For example, barbers do not have Pimps. Well, a prostitute needs a Pimp for protection and law enforcement. A barber can refer to the police for any incident with a customer, but for the illegal prostitute, someone else must do the enforcement. The Pimp fills the void that the police leave. It could enforce laws against Johns who do not pay, Johns that break the terms of the agreement in any form, an overly drunk John that is misbehaving, or just protect against any dangerous thing that may happen in the underground scene. The prostitute is helpless in the dark world of the black market. The Pimp is the one who protects her.

So now the black market consists of Pimps that have prostitutes under them. Pimps will then compete for territory with other Pimps, which equals violence. This is because the neighborhoods in which prostitutes can roam are limited. Combined with the prospects of little competition due to illegality, this makes for a high-stakes fight over territory. Regular pizza parlors also fight for territory, as any business does, but they do it by using money. The rent of a store downtown will be higher than that of a desolate store on an empty street. The competitors hash out their territorial disputes by bidding on rent. In the black market, the disagreement is hashed out with guns and knuckles.

Such a strong dependence on Pimps leaves prostitutes open for exploitation. The Pimps are there to protect the prostitutes against aggressive Johns, but who will protect the prostitutes from Pimps? It's common for Pimps to beat up their prostitutes. Pimps take large cuts from revenue. Some Pimps are also known to hook their prostitutes on drugs to increase their dependence on the Pimp. Just as gangs sell drugs smuggled across borders, the Pimps sell sex-trafficked women. And the same way gangs target teens to be their corner dealers, Pimps target vulnerable girls from troubled neighborhoods. The problems with prostitution, just like the case with drugs, stem from it operating in a black market.

Gambling

Perhaps gambling is the most favored vice. There aren't many people who would condemn their friends' Vegas trip. So why is it illegal?

Gambling can surely be addictive, but as we have discussed, people should be allowed to make their own choices in a free society. It is hard to even think of ways that a third party might be affected by gambling. Unfortunately, the fact of the matter is that gambling is illegal, and situations similar to those with drugs and prostitution arise in the illegal gambling market.

There is no need to repeat these similar points anymore. We understand the essence of it. When something is made illegal, it does not disappear; it just makes its way to the black market. The consequence of any good or service moving to the black market is increased violence, stemming from the need to enforce contracts. With drugs, we had gangs; with prostitutes, we had pimps; and with illegal gambling, we have the so-called loan sharks and debt collectors.

In this section, we want to emphasize a separate point. States ban all private gambling institutions but then operate a state lottery. The hypocrisy is disturbing. Won't any point made in favor of outlawing private gambling apply to government-operated gambling as well? If the state was just going to operate its own games of luck, closing casinos had nothing to do with the moral issues or the addiction potential of gambling.

A state-owned gambling monopoly has some negative consequences. Since the government is the only allowed entity to operate a lottery, it can set the odds significantly in favor of the house. In a free market, consumers would naturally prefer lotteries or any gambling games that offer the highest chances of winning. Obviously, the house also has to make money to cover expenses, so there would be a limit to how much a casino can let the customers win. But ultimately, the payout rates would gravitate to the highest possible amount without the casino losing money: to a happy equilibrium between what the gamblers want and what the casinos want.

However, since the government operates as a monopoly, there is no competition to raise the payouts to what would favor the players. For example, in a blackjack game in Las Vegas, the odds are such that for every $100 bet, you lose $0.50. However, if you bet $100 on the state lottery, you lose between $20 to $40. The state collects 40 to 80 times what a blackjack game collects! In other words, the state is guilty of what it always blames corporations for doing: exploiting customers. The unfortunate thing is that society's low-income members are the overwhelming purchasers of state lotteries. The state reveals its true face by, on the one hand, exploiting its most vulnerable citizens and, on the other hand, asking those very same citizens to give it more power. Supposedly, to protect them against the rich.

CHAPTER 12

Spending For The Common Good

Basic Needs Are Not Any Different

At this point, it should be clear that regulation does more harm than good. However, although some people might accept deregulating commerce in general, they will have a problem when it comes to basic needs, healthcare or education. These are critical matters to leave to the free market.

Actually, the truth is that if an issue is critical, that should be precisely why it should be left to the free market. Certainly, we don't want the people running the DMV and Post Office to be running hospitals and schools. As we keep saying repeatedly, the people in the government are regular people. They will not magically solve problems in a way private citizens cannot. We have consistently shown how the solutions implemented by the government are worse and cost more.

However, maybe people do not mean that the government should run health care or education. Perhaps they think private companies should still take care of basic human needs, but they should be heavily regulated, or they shouldn't be for profit.

Regarding regulation, all that was explained earlier applies to companies for basic needs as well. What we always want is more competition in an industry. Instead of regulating with strict rules that deter competition, the government should step out of the way of businesses trying to provide basic needs. For example, what we now have in healthcare is an elite group of insurance companies, healthcare providers, drug companies, and medical schools, with regulations on who can sell what, operate where, sell to whom, etc. As a result, it is extremely difficult for new competition to disrupt any component of the healthcare industry.

Regarding profits, it is exactly profits that drive people into any industry. The fact that something is profitable, as explained before, is a signal from the market that society would like this problem to be solved. Entrepreneurs compete with one another to offer a higher quality solution at a lower price, meaning everything gets cheaper and better. This is all thanks to profit.

Perhaps the worry is that the price of these basic human needs would be very high if the companies were driven by profit since consumers could not go without purchasing their needs. This might be the case if there was no competition, but in the free market, there is competition. This means that if one company tries to up-charge customers, its competitors would swoop in and take the market share. There is a race to offer the highest quality product for the lowest price. If all competitors agree to charge higher as a pact, a new company can enter the market and take all the customers by offering lower prices. We had already analyzed this scenario. It was called collusion. Collusion is disrupted as soon as new entrepreneurs enter the market. So, the critical issue is not that companies are profiting. That is a good thing that promotes innovation and lowers prices. The problem is again a lack of competition.

Basic needs are not different than other market products. If the market creates excellent solutions for all our other needs, why would the most critical needs be any different? Of course, they won't be unless the government prevents competition.

Proof From Real Life

If you were born into a society in which the government took care of feeding people—since food is a necessity, what would you think if people said, let's privatize food? Perhaps we would see lots of protests and objections to being able to profit from selling food. Those who want to privatize food would be seen as evil greedy capitalists.

What is the reality now? Certainly, a hungry person would pay multiples more for food than something like a TV, but is that the case? Why isn't food extremely expensive the same way healthcare is? Are large corporations withholding food and making us beg for it? Quite the contrary; a significant amount of food is wasted. This is often pointed to as a failure of capitalism, but actually, this highlights the success of capitalism. Food used to be such a precious commodity, but now we can produce so much of it that it expires before we can even eat it. People used to die of starvation not that long ago, but now obesity is a bigger problem.

Think about the extremely high-quality water that just flows from your tap. Kings of the previous centuries could not even drink water as clean as that. But you even shower and flush your toilet with this top-notch water. Imagine if you turned on the tap and freshly brewed Caramel Macchiato flowed out, but you valued it like it was nothing: washing your car with it, pouring it on your plants, putting it in plastic balloons to throw at one another. That is what a past king would think about your water usage. The point is that, despite being a basic need, water has become cheap and abundant. We live in an age of plenty, all thanks to capitalism.

The critical understanding here is that just because a good or service is an essential human need does not mean the companies will turn evil and exploit consumers. Competition keeps prices low and quality high, and the government is the only thing in the way of competition. What determines if a necessity will be abundant and cheap is not whether it is fundamental to human survival; it is whether the market that provides that need is free.

* * *

Some readers may have heard of agricultural subsidies. Since practically every industry is regulated today, there was no alternative basic resource to give as an example. Therefore, what must be explained now is why the subsidies are not why food is plenty.

Say corn is $5, and you have $5 in your pocket. That means you can buy one corn. Now the government intends to subsidize corn to bring its price down to $4. It takes a dollar from you and gives it to the farmer so he can sell the corn for a dollar less. Realistically that dollar erodes as it makes its way through the bureaucracy but suppose perfect efficiency. The farmer takes the $1 subsidy and lowers the price of corn to $4, but that $1 came from your pocket; therefore, now you also have $4. Again, you can buy one corn.

Unless the actual supply of corn goes up, it will not be more affordable. Since the government can only take money from one and give it to another, it cannot make food more abundant. Only the producers in the market can do that, and they do that the most efficiently when the market is free.

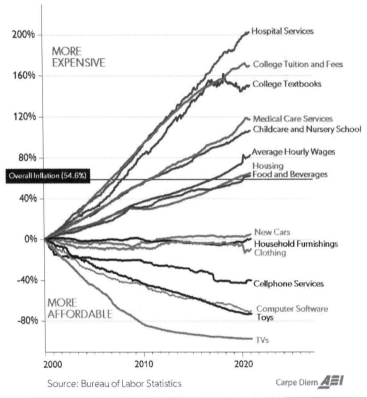

Figure 12.1: Comparing Price changes in common goods and services[5]

This chart shows the prices of many products. Notice that those the government takes part in are all going up, and those the government leaves to the free market are all going down. The following two chapters will show that the healthcare and education industries are the furthest from free markets one can get, which is why price increases are especially drastic in those industries.

Had the cost of any item only kept up with inflation, it would have risen by 54.6%. But what the chart shows is that the price of clothing, cellphone services, computer software, toys, TVs, etc., in fact, went down. This is because there is a high amount of competition in those industries, as opposed to the highly regulated healthcare and education industries. Regardless of whether a good or service is a necessity or not, the free market leads to lower prices, which benefits especially poor people.

Healthcare

Healthcare is a sensitive issue because lives are involved. Most people who would generally be in favor of free markets even cannot accept a free-market healthcare model because of the fact that human lives are at stake. It's not like a case where you are shopping for a car, and if it's too expensive, you look for alternatives. Without fixing your health, you will either live a substandard life or maybe not live at all. When the alternative to not having healthcare is so dire, people think having a free market is evil, greedy, and immoral. They do not want healthcare to be something only the rich can afford but instead something everyone has.

Of course, this exactly is what free-market advocates want as well. Who would not want everyone to be healthy? The disagreement amongst society is about the method by which we can create the healthiest society. This chapter will show that the healthcare industry's problems all stem from government intervention and that a free-market approach, as it always does, will give rise to high-quality, low-cost solutions that especially benefit lower-income people.

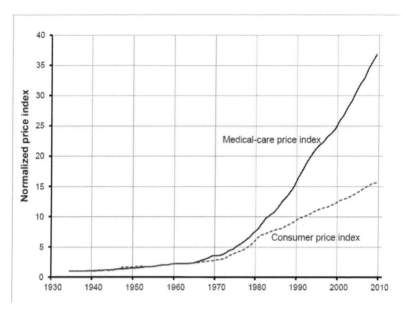

Figure 12.2: An Indexed Comparison of Health Care Inflation and Consumer Price Index in the U.S. from 1935 to 2009 (Source: U.S. Census 2013)[6]

The U.S. spends more than any other country on healthcare on a per capita basis. In 2018, the annual healthcare spending of the average OECD country was $3994 per capita, adjusted for purchasing power. The United States spent $10,586 per capita. The $10,586 is made up of the $8949 spent by the government and the $1637 spent out of pocket by the people. So every time you spend a dollar on healthcare, the government spends about six extra dollars. Citizens do not see this $8949 paid by the government on their behalf and believe we need the government to spend more.[7] We spend more each year, much more than other countries, and our problems persist. Clearly, our problems do not arise from too little government spending.

Quite the opposite is true, actually. Figure 12.2 shows the cost of medical procedures in general compared to the Consumer Price Index (CPI), an index tied to the price of everyday goods and services. It can be seen very clearly that the medical-care price index deviated from the CPI drastically after 1965, which is the year Medicare began. That indicates that the government's involvement in healthcare is the culprit for high prices. Look at the chart closely. Was healthcare not a "basic human need" before 1965? Why would healthcare costs stop following the same trend as most other consumer goods? Healthcare is like any other industry. Its prices would not have skyrocketed if it were not for the government.

But you have always been told the opposite. You likely believe that we have a free market in healthcare, and that is why the prices are so high. You have been told that the prices would be even higher if it were not for the government. Perhaps you do understand that the free market lowers prices generally, but you think that it is not sufficient to extrapolate the success of the free market in other industries to healthcare because perhaps healthcare is unique and should be considered as a specific case study. In that case, let us go into detail and see exactly how and why healthcare is such an issue in the U.S.

No Free Market On The Supply Side

What is an Unnatural Supply Limitation?

Supply and demand are the basics of economics, and they are simple to understand. Demand is how much people want something, and supply is how much there is or that thing. Prices increase when more people want something and vice versa. Prices also increase when there is less of something because people compete for a smaller quantity and vice versa. That is all you need to know to understand this subsection.

Sometimes there is a natural limitation in supply. If the supply of a product suddenly goes down, the price will go up, but this is not necessarily a bad thing. The price is just the voice of the market. It is like a window into the reality of the global market. For example, say the supply of boots is suddenly halved, and the price consequently surges. This is the way of society making a public broadcast to all participants and effectively saying, "Listen, we don't have a lot of these. If you don't really need it, don't buy it now." This message is delivered through the market via price signals. It is a naturally arising limitation, and it is good to let the market speak because this way, only those who really need the boots, like firefighters, search and rescue teams, etc., will buy them. There is no way around a natural supply limitation other than producing more of the product.

For example, if the government comes in and sets a price ceiling (a maximum price that boots can be sold at), then those essential workers who really need the boots will not be able to get them. This is because by setting a price ceiling, the government does not magically bring more boots into existence and lower prices that way. Instead, it lowers the price by decree, which leads to those who actually need the boots not being able to obtain them. This follows from the fact that everyone wants to buy at an artificially lowered price, but the reason for the high price was the fact that there were not enough boots to go around. Reality has not changed. There still is a shortage of boots. If everyone tries to get some, they will run out before the essential workers can get their hands on some. There is no way around a natural supply limitation other than actually producing more of the goods demanded.

In the healthcare industry, the prices are not high because of natural supply constraints. If that were the case, there would be no way around it like we just discussed. The prices are high because of unnecessary limitations to supply, alongside many other reasons. The supply in many healthcare industry segments is low due to unnecessary reasons. What do we mean by unnecessary? Necessary reasons would be those that stem from the basic principle that we have limited resources. So, for example, the supply of movie tickets is naturally limited because there are a limited number of seats. The supply of corn a farmer can grow each year is naturally limited because he has limited land. However, if the government declares the maximum number of corn plants one can grow to be 10,000 plants, then the supply is unnecessarily limited. Or, if permission must be obtained to produce corn, and that permission is seldom granted, the supply would be unnecessarily limited. So let's now see how such practices are prevalent in the healthcare industry.

Problem 1: Artificial Doctor Limitations

The American Medical Association (AMA) convinced Congress that the country had too many substandard medical schools, which went on to produce unqualified doctors. Congress consequently shut down these schools, leading to a 30% reduction in doctor supply over 30 years. Since 1980, the AMA has only allowed a handful of new medical schools to open. Furthermore, they have issued warnings of there being too many physicians, convincing Congress to limit its funding of residencies to 100,000 a year. Since no one, including foreign doctors who are well experienced in their own countries, can practice medicine in the U.S. without completing their residency and obtaining a license, we now face a doctor shortage.[8]

To be clear, the issue here is not about the fact that a license is issued to practice medicine, nor about the idea that medical schools should be up to standard. Society would undoubtedly desire doctors and medical schools to be qualified. Instead, the issue is about the artificial limitation of doctors and medical schools using the legislative powers of Congress. This creates the state-backed monopoly we mentioned in previous chapters that regulations always lead to. Essentially then, an elite group inside the healthcare industry, in alliance with Congress, gets to decide how many medical schools can exist and how many doctors can be licensed to practice each year.

The monopoly enables medical schools to charge ridiculously high tuition since students have no alternative. We said that an exploitative business could not exist in a free market because all consumers would then be drawn to its competitor. If the competitors colluded with the exploitative business and raised prices to extreme levels, new competitors would enter the market and save the consumers. But that cannot happen if the existence of new competition is limited using the power of the government.

Once the students graduate and become doctors, they must charge high prices to patients to recoup medical school costs. So it is important to mention here that doctors themselves are not to blame here. The medical schools make this choice on their behalf. Since the medical schools are aware of their monopoly, they increase their tuition and leave doctors no choice but to raise their prices. A doctor is only trying to make up the money put into getting a degree from a medical school. The choice to jack up prices has been made on behalf of the doctor by the medical school. The blame lies on the medical schools and the AMA, but more importantly, Congress for putting this system in place.

The Need to Enforce Standards

Perhaps, though, you might say that there is some merit to the system because it prevents just anyone from opening up a medical school or becoming a doctor. The current system indeed provides some sort of standards enforcement, but an exploitative monopoly is not the only way to achieve this. The central matter here is that society wants to trust doctors. We can have the free market do this as well. We know that the free market can provide for any need of society, which also includes the need to enforce standards. We already went into how the free market can provide trust under the regulations chapter, but let's specifically think about the healthcare market as well.

Let's break down the mechanics of this market. There are essentially three players: the doctors, the people who practice medicine; the educators, the people who train doctors; and the verifiers, the people who verify that such and such doctor is qualified. Consumers trust the verifiers to ensure that the doctors are qualified, and the educators train doctors to become qualified. All we need to do to fix the shortage is to liberate the markets of verifiers and educators. The liberation will disrupt the current monopoly and stop them from controlling how many doctors are licensed, in other words, verified, and how many medical schools, in other words, educators, can exist.

A free market of educators means that anyone can open a doctor training facility, which is what a medical school is, just like how anyone can open a test prep center. Doctors do not prefer a doctor training facility that is not good at its job, and consequently, it goes out of business. What determines whether a doctor training facility is good at its job is whether it can train doctors well enough to satisfy the requirements of the verifiers. Therefore, verifiers play a crucial role in the market. They are the people consumers practically put their trust in.

Each year, the verifier companies will compete with one another to prepare a better test that genuinely measures a student's medicinal capabilities, just like what the ACT and SAT do for high school students. However, obviously, the verifiers will need to be a lot stricter on the prospective doctors than the SAT and ACT are on high schoolers. The verifiers can subject doctors to real-life simulations, fake crisis moments, months-long hospital experiences with qualified doctors, etc. Verifier companies can choose to incorporate any of the current barriers to becoming a doctor, add more requirements if they find them necessary, or take some out if they think it's unnecessary.

But why would any of these companies look out for consumers? What is stopping a verifier from certifying a doctor too easily? It's a free market, right? That is true. But no consumer will respect their certificate, meaning no doctor will be interested in earning that certification. So, for example, there may be an easy college entrance exam as an alternative to the SAT, and you may have gotten a full score on that exam. That test company is attempting to act as a verifier for your abilities. However, no college respects that test because it is not actually good at verifying the skills of the student; it's too easy. Therefore, no student takes the test, and the verifier goes out of business. There is pressure from the market on the verifier companies to be tough on the doctors and only qualify the ones who are well-equipped to practice medicine.

In the end, educating and verifying, whether it's by the free market or government-approved agencies, are just actions performed by a group of people. There is no reason why a group of government-approved people would do a job better than a group of people in the free market. In fact, the free market is supreme because of the competition that constantly forces people to improve and the freedom to choose that consumers have. This means that we can comfortably liberate the markets and solve the shortage.

In conclusion, one of the problems in the healthcare industry is the artificially low supply of doctors. This is precisely due to the markets not being free because there is no such thing as a long-term shortage in a free market. The free market is the voice of society, and the shortage is the society crying for more of the thing in short supply. Therefore there must be something preventing the supply from increasing, which we saw was the AMA. This means that we need to liberate the market for doctors, educators, and verifiers, and we need not worry about this because the free market is supreme due to the competition that constantly forces people to improve and the freedom to choose that consumers have.

In the end, educating and verifying, whether it's by the free market or government-approved agencies, are just actions performed by a group of people. There is no reason why a group of government-approved people would do a job better than a group of people in the free market.

We need to produce more doctors to lower prices, but that means more medical schools need to open up, and more residencies need to be allowed. And that can't happen unless Congress allows for the monopoly to be disrupted.

Problem 2: Health Care Provider Regulations

Hospitals are another part of the healthcare industry in which supply is artificially limited. The government regulates: when, what, and who may open new healthcare facilities. It can cost great sums and up to 10 years to get a health facility going. The regulations also don't stop once you open the facility either. The administrative costs of hospitals are near a third of all their expenses. All these high costs reflect in the final price. Furthermore, in addition to burdening existing hospitals, regulation, as we already know, deters new competition from coming in and facilitates the big players to eat up the small players. This paves the path to monopolization.

In this section, we will talk about a specific hospital regulation. No matter what you generally think of regulations, you will likely agree that this one is ridiculous. It is something called a "certificate of need," and it must be obtained to open a new hospital. This certificate is granted if there is a need for a hospital to be built. But the free market is already a certificate of need. If a hospital has patients coming in, then it satisfies a need. If the demand is not enough, the hospital cannot pay the bills and disappears. In every industry, the free market automatically acts as a certificate of need. Who would invest millions of dollars, go through all the other regulatory struggles, open a hospital where there is no need, and go bankrupt months later? Plus, doesn't the government always claim to pass regulations to protect the poor from evil corporations. Why protect the evil corporations from building hospitals where there is no need? Let them build and fail.

To understand how senseless of a regulation this is, apply it to all businesses. For example, imagine if your local gym had to prove that there is a need for a gym in this neighborhood. Or apply it to yourself and, say you wanted to be a musician, think about having to prove that there is a need for musicians. How would to even prove that, and what kind of authoritarian society is that? As we discussed before, no single person knows whether there is or isn't a need for something. No one knows which resource should be allocated where, which businesses should open where, or serve whom. Individual people make decisions, and they coordinate their actions using feedback from the free market.

So then, what is the reason we have the certificate of need regulations? Well, that is an interesting question. For a hospital to get a certificate of need, it applies with appropriate documents, and a committee decides if there is a need. And who is on the committee, you might ask? The existing hospitals! Exactly. You ask the current hospitals in the area whether you could operate next to them, and you know, force them to compete and lower prices. What do you suppose the answer is?

Problem 3: Prescription Medication Regulations

As we said, if there is a need for regulation, the free market can provide for this need. When it comes to prescription medication, society wants assurance of efficacy, safety, and quality. Let's call this triplet "X," so X = [efficacy, safety, and quality]. People want to buy X, and they want to get it fast and get it for cheap. Of course, since the government is in charge, society receives a not-so-good X by spending more money and waiting longer. The problems in the prescription medication sector stem from this fact. FDA approval for a new drug, or anything for that matter, like a new prosthetic or medical device, takes at least a couple of years, loads of paperwork, and huge sums of money. When the issue involves human health, the costs of dealing with regulations and delays in time are paid with human lives. This section will explore the problems in the U.S. prescription medication industry.

First, from a time perspective, a lengthy approval process means that during the unnecessarily protracted approval process, those who may benefit from using some medication are deprived of this benefit. We are not talking about merely pain relief benefits, although that is still important. We are talking about serious medications that save lives. A famous example is how even though Beta-Blockers were already approved and used in Europe, Americans could not buy them for years. The lag in FDA approval of these drugs cost 250,000 lives alone. Similarly, a five-year delay in the introduction of Septra, an antibiotic, was estimated to have cost 80,000 lives.[9]

After tragic stories of individuals traveling abroad to use approved treatments in other countries, the "Right to Try" act was signed into law in 2018. It allowed terminally ill patients to access experimental therapies that the FDA has not yet approved. However, this still did not fix the issue for the millions of people who do not benefit from this law since they are not terminally ill. These people still cannot use promising medication to save their lives or greatly reduce their discomfort.

Now let's take a look at the problem of high costs. Say you are a farmer, and the government mandates that you must get approval for every crop you intend to grow, which will cost $1000. If you want to grow potatoes, you must get approval costing $1000. If you want to grow corn, you must get another approval costing $1000, and so on. You know that at least 100 people want to buy potatoes, so you get authorization to grow potatoes and grow one potato for $1. It would not make sense to sell this potato for any less than $11.

Even though each potato costs $1 to grow, you spent $1000 on the government approval and divided this cost evenly amongst the 100 people, resulting in $10 extra from each buyer. You are not evil for doing this; you must do this. Otherwise, you will lose money until you cannot farm again, and then society would have no potatoes at all. Certainly, $11 potatoes are better than no potatoes at all. So you see, the reason for the high potato price here is not the farmer's greed; it's the $1000 authorization cost.

This is precisely the situation with prescription drugs. The costly approval process and the research and development costs reflect in the final price. Each stage of bringing a drug to market, starting with development, testing, and approval, up until the final point of sale in which, who can sell, what they can sell, how much they can sell, where they can sell, to whom they can sell, etc., is heavily regulated.

That explains why drugs are generally expensive. Now, let's explore why sometimes a specific medication is costly. Consider the same farmer, but now suppose that only one person in society wants a particular fruit. It is not that hard to grow this fruit; it still costs $1. Maybe it will take some time and money to research how to grow this crop specifically, but it's not too bad overall. However, there is still that pesky $1000 approval cost. Unless the final price of the fruit is $1001, the farmer cannot grow this. In this case, the approval costs are only paid by a single person, so the final price of the crop is much larger.

With prescription drugs, this happens when a subset of society has a very rare disease. The drug company either does not attempt to make a drug for this disease since the patients cannot pay the high costs, or they still do it, but the final price is very high. Nowadays, bringing a new drug to market costs $2.8 Billion.[10]

Drug companies will not get off so easy, though. They certainly have their offenses too. Under the regulation chapter, we went over the effects of regulation and understood how it leads to monopolies. We saw that the high costs of abiding by regulation do not affect big companies the same way it burdens smaller companies. Eventually, the small companies are either bought up by the big ones or go bankrupt. Additionally, no new company can enter the industry either due to the high barriers to entry imposed by regulation and the risk due to the already huge company's advantage. Big Pharma is no exception to this. Not just one company but a few giant corporations mutually benefit from the corrupt government and regulatory agencies. This monopoly status they hold allows them to charge exorbitant prices, more than enough to recoup development and regulatory costs.

Again, though, you must realize that this is thanks to the government. Government regulations increase drug prices by first making it costly to bring a drug to market and then by enabling monopoly pricing. The result is that all drugs are more expensive, and some niche drugs are especially expensive or are not even produced. More costly drugs mean fewer people can buy them, so more people die or remain in discomfort, and suppression of some drug innovations implies that some people can never even receive their cure.

Finally, let's address why the drugs that American companies make are cheaper in other countries. The governments of these countries put a price ceiling for which the drug company must sell below. This prevents the drug companies from utilizing their monopolistic advantage to charge extra high prices. This is good. We don't want corporations to exploit customers. But slashing regulations is still a better strategy than implementing a price ceiling. Cutting regulations promotes competition, which prevents monopolization. However, the monopoly was only part of the reason for high prices. The price ceiling does not retroactively reduce the regulatory cost of developing the drug (the $1000 approval cost for the farmer). The only way to reduce that cost would be to reduce the regulations.

What happens next? The company has to make up for this cost somehow. Just like in the potato example, if there are 100 people who want the potato, the cost of the potato will be $1 to manufacture the potato + $10 to get approval, split evenly between the 100 people. If 50 of the 100 people are protected by a price ceiling, and will only pay a maximum of $2, then the other 50 must pay extra in order to cover the $1000 cost. The protected group only pays $1 towards their fair share of the approval costs. Therefore, the price for the unprotected 50 people rises to $20 because they have to pay what the protected crowd did not.

This ends up being Americans. Foreign countries do not pay for their share of the development costs. If America also had a price ceiling. Then the drug would not exist because there would be no place where the company could make up the cost that went into developing the drug. So, in conclusion, it is true that drug companies overcharge by abusing their monopoly status, but they have some actual costs that come from regulations, and a ceiling cannot undo those costs.

No Free Market On The Demand Side

In the previous section, we discussed the problems on the supply side of healthcare: medical schools, hospitals, drug companies, etc. Now let's take a look at the demand side, or in other words, the consumer side.

Recall the mechanism of the free market. Consumers desire to receive something of value in exchange for their money. Their goal is to get the most value for as little money as possible. Given this fact, the suppliers are under constant competition to reduce unnecessary costs, find new ways to lower prices, innovate, become more efficient, and ultimately deliver the highest quality product for the lowest price. How come then, when it comes to healthcare, the prices are so high? It might surprise you that there is no free market on the demand side either.

Problem 1: Post-Pricing

Let's say you want to rent a place to live. You would typically check out a couple of places, ask for prices, and begin due diligence. You would figure out some questions like: Are the amenities included? How does the quality compare to similarly priced apartments? How much more am I willing to pay for a place near downtown? What you are doing in this process is hunting for the highest quality for the lowest price. If you and many others looking to rent apartments do not ask these questions, the market will not function properly.

The landlord wants to get as much money as possible for his apartment, and the renter wants to get as much quality as possible for his money. Together, they settle at an equilibrium. There is no limit to what the landlord can charge, as he would be happy with more money. However, the renter's demand for high quality for a low price keeps the lid on prices. If the landlord unfairly prices his place too high, the renter would find a landlord that reasonably prices his home. However, if the renter stops doing his due diligence or stops caring, the landlord can get away with charging whatever he can.

It seems odd that anyone wouldn't care, though. Who would not want to get the most quality for the lowest price? Every consumer is clearly interested in keeping as much of his hard-earned dollars as possible.

Well, healthcare works in such a way that the consumer does not even know the price of any procedure he will undergo until after the fact. Let me ask you, how much does it cost to get sutures, a CAT Scan, or blood work done? Do you know the actual cost of any medical procedure? In fact, even if you asked your doctor, he would say that he either does not know or that he could not tell you. Imagine renting a place but not knowing the price until after you moved out, at which point the landlord charged you a million dollars. What options do you have? You have already stayed at the place for a year. In the healthcare industry, prices for most procedures are determined after the fact, which means consumers are not shopping around for better prices, allowing hospitals to charge what they want. This is why the cost of the same exact procedure in the same city can be radically different.[11]

Problem 2: Insurance-Hospital Alliance

American hospitals are notorious for charging excessively high prices for things like a tiny bit of ultrasonic gel or for the ability to hold your baby after giving birth. Looking into the details of how the payment system works, we will see that the deeper issue here is the cooperation of hospitals and insurance companies to maintain an exploitative system. Basically, your hospital charges you, let's say, ten times what it needs to charge, and then your insurance company comes and "negotiates" with the hospital on your behalf and lowers the price by 90%. This system locks you into needing an insurance company. Hospitals still make a great profit, insurance companies have locked themselves in between the patient and the hospital, so they're happy, and the consumer is the only loser.

The system is broken. In order to buy an apple, you go to the grocery store and ask for the price. They say go ahead, just eat it; we will bill your friend Steve later. Steve comes up to you later and says that the apple was $15, but he was able to reduce it to $2 because he knows the grocery store owner. You pay Steve some money every month for this service. You are the patient, the grocer is the hospital, and Steve is your insurance. You could've bought the apple from the grocer directly in a free market for $1, but instead, you bought it for $2 and also had to pay monthly premiums to Steve.

Problem 3: User is not the Payer

Let's go through a thought experiment. Your party of 5 friends goes to a restaurant. Before ordering, everyone agrees to only pay for what they order. Everyone looks at the menu and chooses what they think is a good value for the price. You each individually pay, and the total is $100.

Now the next day, the same party meets again, and this time they decide to just split the bill. Initially, you were thinking of ordering a modest soup, but your friend across the table just ordered a fillet-mignon with an extra side of mashed potatoes. Since the check will be split, you will pay for 1/5th of a fillet-mignon while only having a lousy soup to enjoy. You're really getting the dirty end of the stick here, so you also decide to order a nice steak dish. The total cost of everything comes out to be $500 this time.

This is how insurance works. You don't care about the cost of any medical procedure because everyone under your insurance group splits the cost. It doesn't make sense for you to be frugal when you know that the millions of others in your group are probably not as careful as you. You may remember from the basic principles that if one does not pay for a product but is the ultimate user of the product, he only cares about quality and not price. As expected, healthcare in America is high quality but also high priced.

Problem 4: Composition of the Insurance Group

The basis of insurance is to place people in a group, so the costs are spread out. Sometimes you will incur some costs, and sometimes others will. Over your lifetime, it will balance out so that no one takes advantage of the system. It is essentially a pact you make with a group of random people to spread costs over time. However, the members of your group make a difference. For the system to be fair, the groups must be made up of similar individuals.

For example, let's consider car insurance. If one is a good driver, he will incur the costs of reckless drivers in his group. For this reason, the relatively freer market in car insurance compared to health insurance aims to group people by their risk levels. Each car insurer seeks to save their customers money so that they would choose them over their competitors. Therefore, many car insurers place their customers in smaller and smaller buckets based on their risk level, intending to save them as much money as possible. This is why teenagers, those with a history of crashes, those with powerful cars, convertible cars, and even red cars, pay higher rates because the insurance companies place them in a high-risk category. It's not unfair to do so. In fact, it is unfair to do the opposite. Why should responsible drivers be punished with higher rates? People are incentivized to drive carefully because cautious drivers are rewarded with lower rates.

If we had something similar in healthcare, our citizens would care more about their health. It would be easy to group based on even a simple metric such as body fat percentage, which is linked to the greatest killer in this country, heart disease. Such a system would incentivize people to lose weight. We would have a healthier society and save money, but forget grouping based on weight; we cannot even group based on pre-existing conditions. Our system makes it illegal to discriminate against people with existing conditions, which is the equivalent of buying insurance on your car after you crash.

It may be your moral stance that we should not group people like this when it comes to healthcare. You may believe that we are all humans on this planet and should bear the cost of healthcare equally. This is an acceptable belief, but an insurance company that does not group customers could also exist in a free market. Those who subscribe to that ideology can join that insurance company. In addition, you could do the following. Suppose you yourself are healthy but believe that we should not price discriminate against unhealthy people. In that case, nothing in the free market prevents you from donating the excess money you save on your insurance by being a healthy individual to those who are less healthy. Perhaps everyone cannot afford to be that generous, though. Maybe a lower class individual pays attention to his health and does not want to pay for the health expenses of reckless people. Should he not have that right?

The moral argument against price discrimination against unhealthy people is understandable. Evenly splitting the bill, although technically unfair, feels like the virtuous thing to do. However, under that rule, our insurance system does not incentivize anyone to maintain their health, meaning that the bill is much larger at the end of the year. The alternative is to group by health levels and incentivize staying healthy. Each year people would try to stay healthy to lower their risk level. This way, the people would get healthier, and the bill would get smaller.

Education

The United States has been spending multiple times more than it used to on public K-12 schools, but the scores on tests are still flat. We increase funding for public schools each year and get little in return, and we seem to believe that the answer is more spending. Most likely, citizens are not even aware that we spend more and more each year and get little improvements, but politicians tell us that more spending is the answer, so we believe.

When it comes to universities, we have decent quality, but the costs are skyrocketing, which we saw in Figure 12.1. More and more kids are being crushed by student debt each day.

So again, you will see in this chapter that the pattern is clear; the further we deviate from free-market principles, the worse the outcomes become.

K-12 Education

Let's start with K-12 education, which is the schools up until but not including universities. What kind of system do we have in place here? The public schools get direct funding from the government, and students are just assigned to schools in their district based on location. So on the supply side, the schools are not incentivized to offer quality since their funding is loosely dependent on performance, if at all. And on the demand side, students have no choice in what school they go to, so they cannot pressure the school to offer better quality education. This is the primary problem. In a free market, service providers compete for customers, forcing them to lower costs and improve quality. The K-12 education providers do not compete for students; therefore, they have no reason to improve quality and lower prices.

Once again, parents fall into the fallacy of thinking everything the government provides is free. They say, "Well, it's free, and it is better than no education." The issue is that when you think it is free, the benchmark becomes nothing. However, it is not free. The government does not create anything; they tax citizens and spend on their behalf. Education comes from the taxes you pay, usually property taxes. Even if you rent your home, you pay these taxes because your landlord pays the taxes on your behalf and passes on the costs to you by increasing your rent accordingly. So, we get the same situation we always do, where the taxpayer is grateful to the government for a "free" service and is unaware of what he would have if the government would step out of the way.

Nothing else in our society works this way, and it's for a reason: it does not make any sense. Why should the government take money from you in the form of taxes, spend it on your behalf on schools, and then assign you to one based on how close you are to the school? It is not just completely unnecessary but, in fact, hurtful because the true payer of the money, the taxpayer, is taken out of the buying process; the parent of the student loses his voice.

Still, it's hard to challenge this system without others assuming you want only the rich to be able to get educated. It is generally the reaction against free-market principles. But time and again, we saw that it is, in fact, the government's involvement in industries that leads to high prices and unaffordability. Taking the government out of industries would lower costs and make the products more affordable, benefiting poor people the most. This has been the case every single time, but still, it is hard to get past the rhetoric pushed by the politicians and connect to the rationality within people.

If we just took food as an example, since it is also a basic human need, and applied the education model, the undeniable foolishness would be apparent. The government shall tax you a set amount each year, then allocate that money after passing it through its bureaucracy to a grocer. Later, assign you to the closest grocer in your area. In fact, if this is the better way to run things, why not add housing to the mix? Let's also tax you an extra amount and spend this on a local housing complex on your behalf and just give you a spot there. Then, we should tax some more and allocate it to a local car factory nearby, which simply gives you a car. How about you just pay a 100% tax so the government can spend on your behalf and allocate you your needs. What do we get when we do this? Communism. The issue with command economies in general, which communism is, is the impossibility of managing an economy from the top-down. The free market is efficient because individuals have their best interests in mind, and they make local decisions, which propagate through the signals in the market. You see that our approach to public education is what a communist country would do. If communism fails when applied to the entire economy, it will also fail when applied to only education.

The solution is to have a free-market education system. This means parents pay out of pocket for their schools. However, this does not cost them anything extra. They would merely keep the money that was taxed from them and then spend it on a school of their choice. The keyword here is choice. Because this system gives the students or their parents a choice, the schools have to attract them. Each year they work hard to offer a better education at a lower price.

* * *

So, you may ask, if public schools are of low quality, why don't all parents send their kids to private schools? Some fancy private schools appeal to those who want a bit of luxury and exclusivity and thus cost significant sums of money. However, when looking at ordinary private schools, they do indeed deliver better test scores for less money. The issue is that most people cannot send their kids there because they are already paying for a nearby public school by being taxed for it, whether they want to or not. Therefore, they would need to pay extra for a private school.

Say the family spends $10,000 on the public school via taxes, and the private school is $8,000. The parent would technically save $2,000 by choosing the private option, so he would prefer it. But instead, since there is no choice to opt out of taxes, the family would end up paying $18,000 total to educate their kids if they chose the private option: $10,000 taxed against their will for a service they do not prefer to use, plus the $8000 extra for the private school.

Some states have begun implementing a voucher system to deal with this problem. This is the closest we have gotten to a free market system. The system gives families a voucher to spend on schools, which is technically their own money being handed back to them in the form of a coupon only spendable at a school. The families then pick a school to be the recipient of this voucher. Under this system, the parents first and foremost get to choose a school. This keeps schools accountable. Second, this fixes the double-spending issue mentioned in the above paragraph since the vouchers also apply to private schools. Giving parents the ability to decide which schools get to have their tax dollars should not be a controversial proposition. This is a great program, which we hope to see implemented more.

From a social aspect, one effect of the lack of choice is further inequality, likely the opposite of what the proponents of more funding for public schools want. When an individual is taxed, and the money is spent on the individual's behalf on a particular school, he becomes locked into that school. We also know that private schools are better than public schools because of competition. A rich family can forgo the amount that was spent on their behalf on the public school and still send their child to a better private school. However, the poorer family cannot. The result is worse education for the poor and better for the rich.

The effects of this simple act on a person's life are significant. Better education means a better job, more money, better life. The opposite is true for the poorer person, who will most likely keep voting for policies that increase the intervention of government in the name of "help" but end up worsening inequality.

* * *

Now, let's think about the actual matters your child is getting educated on. What would your reaction be if a stranger told you he was going to change the school curriculum? Probably you would ask what he had in mind? What kind of person is this guy? How would he know what's best for my child? However, do you even know who is in charge of your child's school curriculum now? The government is in charge of education, so you can be assured that qualified people are handling that task, right?

The brains of children are like sponges; they soak up what is given to them right away. Your child likely spends more time in school than he does with you. Likely, you know nothing about what he learns and who he spends time with, and he will be at this institution until the age of 18, 5 out of 7 days, 8 hours every day. If you exclude 8 hours of sleep every day, there are 112 hours in a week. Your child will spend

40 of those in school. For a third of the week, you have no idea what your child is getting indoctrinated in.

Now, if you had a choice over your child's school, wouldn't you ask these crucial questions before sending them there? At the core of it, schooling is indoctrination. You may believe it to be benevolent indoctrination, but it still is indoctrination. Your child goes to an institution for a significant portion of his time, learns what to do and say from figures of authority, and you get no choice over these figures of authority. You may think public schools may not be evil now, but they have the power to do evil if desired. The point here is not to say that public schools are malicious; it is to highlight the importance of choice over a major institution in your child's life.

Higher Education

Unlike in K-12 Education, universities are not automatically allocated students and therefore must compete for them. This means they have to offer better education and a better experience overall. Consequently, it is not surprising that American universities are the best in the world. The problem with universities is not that the quality is bad; it is that the price is unaffordable.

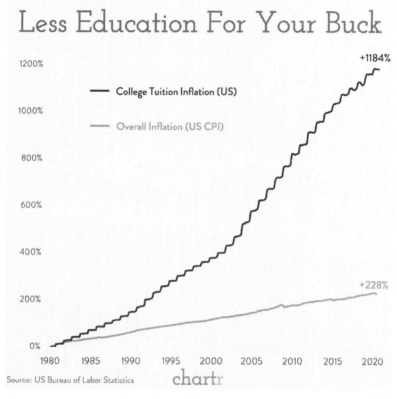

Figure 12.3: Increase in college education cost starting from 1980[12]

Rationally, the cost should actually go down, just like how the price of everything else on the chart is falling. As time goes on, society becomes more efficient, technology develops, infrastructure improves, and therefore all costs go down. That is unless the government steps in. The interference in universities came in the form of student loans backed by the Federal Government. Basically, the government gave a university loan to anyone who wanted one, regardless of their ability to pay it back. As is always the case, this policy sounded better than it actually was. The effect has been skyrocketing costs, meaningless degrees, and a student loan bubble.

Before government-backed loans, a student would either have their parents pay for the degree or borrow from a private lender. And some students could even put themselves through college by working a few hours on the side. In either scenario, there would be some sort of cost-benefit analysis done by the student, parent, or private lender before paying for college.

What is meant by a cost-benefit analysis? Well, what is university education at its core? It is a skill set that a worker adds on to increase his productivity. So one shops for a university education the same way one shops for any other tool that increases his productivity. For example, suppose your job is to hammer down nails. Does it make sense to buy a nail gun? Maybe. How much faster will you be with the nail gun, and how much extra income will that generate for you? Now, is that extra income worth the cost of a nail gun? Probably, so you should go ahead and buy it. Or, suppose you are a waiter. If you learn Spanish, you estimate that you can impress 20% of your tables each night and thus generate some more income from tips. But, is the extra income worth the cost of Spanish lessons? Perhaps. Finally, suppose you want to become a private pilot. You calculate how much it would cost to earn your license and compare this to how much income you will generate as a private pilot. Then, you sign up for classes only if their costs are justified by the income you will earn.

All these examples demonstrate the experience of buying tools with the ultimate goal of making more money. The analysis performed by the buyers of tools keeps a lid on prices because no tool buyer would buy a tool that costs more than the extra income it will bring in.

University prices remained low when the market was functioning this way. Even if the high schooler were not competent to make a proper economic investment decision, his private lender would think on his behalf. The lender's goal would be to analyze the high schooler well and ensure that this kid is not taking on a massive loan for a major that would not earn him a job. But suppose the private lender became a permanent drunk. He began issuing loans to everyone who wanted one. Any high schooler wanting to study anything received a loan from the lender. What would happen?

Since that exactly is what the federal government did by guaranteeing student loans, we can answer the question by looking at the situation now. The universities raised prices as the lender no longer cared about the cost vs. future-income dynamic. The goal became to sucker into college as many people as possible, which gave rise to meaningless degrees with no real-world application. "Family and Consumer Sciences" major, with a median salary within five years of graduation of $32,000, ranks the worst paying college major.[13] To put that salary into better perspective, let's view it as an hourly rate, which comes out to about $15 per hour. So a $250,000 "tool" gives the buyer the same income after four years as pretty much any person working a standard job. It is the equivalent of paying a quarter-million dollars and waiting four years in line at a hardware store, only to see that the "supreme tool" you have been waiting for is a regular hammer.

What caused this problem was the government's bad investments. Its decision to give anyone a loan, regardless of their ability to pay it back, was exacerbated by the rhetoric they pushed that everyone must be college-educated. So, it was not enough that loans were given to people that could not pay them back; more people were encouraged to become indebted. Everyone does not need a university education for the same reason that everyone does not need a Ph.D. Ultimately, education is a tool that you invest in. If you don't need the tool or its cost exceeds its future benefit, don't buy it.

What we have in our hands now is the immense student debt bubble. Some people would just like to erase away this debt, but that would be unfair to all students who had already paid their debts. On the other hand, it feels indecent to expect payments from students pressured by government propaganda to take on loans and go to college. No one knows what will happen, but hopefully, soon, people will realize that the answer to problems that the government created is not more government; it is free markets.

What Happens to Those Who Can't Pay

Perhaps, after seeing how all the problems in healthcare and education are caused by government intervention, you are ready to accept a free market. You understand that free markets lead to lower prices and higher quality, which would benefit poor people. However, there is likely one last problem you have with freeing the markets. That is the issue of dealing with those who truly cannot afford basic needs even at the low free-market prices. This might compel you to suggest that the government must exist to take care of these people. Essentially, since the politicians will not actually roll up their sleeves and get to work to produce necessary goods and services, this means the following: we must take from the rich and give to the government to spend on behalf of the impoverished.

Right away, though, we can see a few things. First, it would be more efficient to get rid of the government in the middle and have the rich directly give to the poor. That way, one, the bureaucracy wouldn't take part of the money, so more of it would reach the poor, and two, the poor would directly spend their money rather than the government spending on their behalf.

And second, to not break voluntarism, we must not "take" from anyone. No matter how virtuous a cause is, it is not moral to force people to donate to it. But there is good news. People are charitable, so you will not need to force them; they are naturally willing to give. How do we know? The proof is the existence of this chapter. The very fact that you were concerned about the impoverished people in a free market system shows that you care. It would make you happy, for example, to know that a mentally disabled child will live one more year. We don't know exactly how happy it would make you, but if a dollar value were to be attributed to that happiness, it would be greater than zero. Therefore, if a private charity approached you and offered to trade you [the happiness from helping that child] for [some of your money], you would voluntarily accept that transaction.

An objection might be this: "I don't care if rich people are forced. It is their humanitarian duty to donate more than the rest of us. It isn't my responsibility to help the underprivileged as rich people just stockpile their cash." Obviously, this person is okay with using force to take someone's money, also known as theft, if it is committed against a rich person. They will likely not change this belief so let's try another approach. Perhaps we could ease the tensions a bit by getting them not to hate rich people.

First, let's start by saying that there are undoubtedly immoral ways of becoming rich. The first, ironically, is by taking money by force. The only entity in a free market that can legally do this is the government. The second is by forming an alliance with the government and using the force of the government to gain wealth. This happens when a politically connected elite lobbies for regulation that establishes his company as a monopoly.

There are also moral ways of getting rich. In a free market, one makes money by offering a product or service to people in exchange for dollars. That is the only way. Every single dollar earned is voluntarily handed over by the recipient of the product or service precisely because they felt that the exchange was fair and desirable. We must break the paradigm that billionaires are automatically bad people. As long as the transactions are voluntary, there can be no moral objection to how much money a person has accumulated. On the contrary, it means that this person has provided a billion dollars worth of happiness in the form of products or services, for which free individuals have voluntarily chosen to exchange their money. Therefore, we should, in fact, appreciate the sheer number of people they have made happy.

It is crucial to differentiate between the rich who made money fairly versus unfairly. We are against the corrupt corporations who enrich themselves by lobbying the corrupt government as well. But, there is no reason to hate the uncorrupt rich people.

Still, the objection might be that rich people are not using their accumulated wealth to benefit society. You may say, "Fine. They are not as evil as I thought. But still, they can be doing so much with their wealth. Instead, they choose to hoard their cash or do stupid things like recreationally going to space. Meanwhile, poor people are suffering."

New technology, like recreational space flight, is created by rich people, initially for other rich people. This has always been the case, for example, for cell phones, computers, commercial air flights, and more. Because, for a technology to develop, many resources must be committed to its development. A problem with no known solution must be solved, which means failed attempts, lost money, and lots of time. The expenses of all the scientists and engineers have to come out of someone's pocket. That has to be the rich people. Some rich person must have an idea, or a motivated fellow must pitch an idea to a rich person. After a risk-benefit analysis, the project will either be pursued or scrapped. If the project is successful, all the costs of development will be recouped from other rich people by selling the successful product at a high price.

So, contrary to popular belief, rich people do not stockpile their wealth and hoard resources away from society. Instead, they continually invest their savings to create new projects. Of course, some rich people do spend money on luxuries, which they are allowed to do since their money comes from providing something for others. However, the point is that no one hoards their cash. It is either spent, so it disappears, or invested, so it funds new projects.

Even at the initial stages of a project, where only the rich can access the new product, society has benefited. A creative pursuit began and ended with success. Only the affluent members of society will have the new product now, but it is better than no one having it. Let's use cell phones as an example. Even though one may not have personally had a cell phone in the past, he would benefit from others having cell phones because operations would run more efficiently now. If a certain portion of society is more efficient, more and better goods and services will be produced using our limited resources. Certainly, the case is apparent when you are a direct beneficiary of the efficiency. Consider a search and rescue operation. Would you prefer the search and rescue team to have cell phones or not? What about helicopters? You may not personally have one, but you are glad that they exist, right?

Initially, any new product starts off as expensive, and only the rich can buy it. But with time, the competition in the free market lowers prices to where everyone can buy one. When the first cell phone was developed, it proved that the challenge had a solution. After that point, millions jumped on the problem and competed to make cheaper and higher-quality cell phones. At first, the huge, blocky, limited capability cellphones sold for thousands. Now we buy touchscreen phones with apps, GPS, cameras, and thousands of more capabilities for a few hundred dollars. That is how the initial investments by the rich help enrich the poor with time.

Society benefits from innovation. Even when they are expensive and only for the rich at first, they become better and cheaper with time. But, for innovation, we need investment, and for investment, we need large savings. The problems we all want solutions to, like extending the human lifespan, going to other planets, flying cars, or anything futuristic that comes to mind, will need savings to solve. How can we expect new inventions if we take away rich people's savings?

So, clearly, the rich do not squander their money. They put it to productive use. Therefore, the last remaining objection could be this: "Okay. Rich people are not bad people, and they do put their money to productive use. They do help the poor by developing new products or creating competing businesses to lower the costs of existing products. However, why can't they at least contribute a little bit of their money to address the problems of poor people directly? For example, why can't they directly give money each year to programs that help the poor." The answer is, of course, that they do. They practically fund all our social programs. No matter how much the greedy politicians say that the rich do not pay their fair share, the fact of the matter is that the top 3%, those with taxable income (Adjusted Gross Income) of about $250,000, pay more than half the federal taxes. That sounds more than fair, actually. [14]

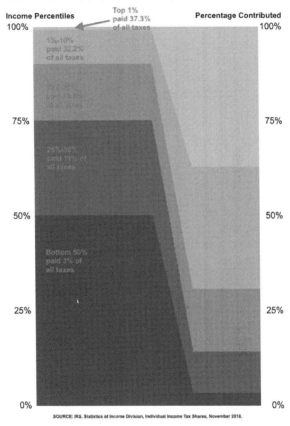

Contributions to the Total Tax Collected from various Income Brackets

Top 1% paid 37.3% of all taxes

Income Percentiles

Percentage Contributed

SOURCE: IRS, Statistics of Income Division, Individual Income Tax Shares, November 2018.

Figure 12.4: Contributions to the yearly "Income Tax Pie" coming from various Income Brackets [14]

Now knowing all this, let's revisit our initial objective. This chapter aimed to solve the issue of providing for those who cannot provide for themselves. This meant that fundamentally, money would need to come from some people and flow to others. We said that a charity system would align with our principle of voluntarism. However, we acknowledged that some in society would not find charity sufficient and would demand to take money from the rich to help the poor. It would not matter to them that this would be stealing. The fact that they would be stealing from the rich would justify their immoral action because they have a profound hatred for the rich. Or, perhaps, if it isn't hate that compels them, it is a belief that the burden to help the underprivileged falls on the rich.

We have demonstrated that the rich are not evil unless they make their money by corrupting the government. The amount of money they have is equal to the happiness they have provided to others. We also showed how they invest their money to fund the creation of new technology, which propels humanity forward. Finally, we highlighted that they already pay a majority of the taxes. So now, we invite those who want to tax the rich to shift their focus from the people who give the funds to the people who spend the funds. Perhaps the issue is not that we do not tax the rich enough.

In 2021, the federal government spent $6,800,000,000,000, that is $6.8 Trillion. To put that into perspective, that is $0.78 Billion, not each month, not each day, but each hour. With the current federal government we have, even if we tax 100% of the wealth, not even income but the entire net worth of someone worth $1 billion, we would only fund the federal government for about 77 minutes. And this calculation does not even include state and local governments. It is only the Federal Government, which is the government that the Constitution intended to keep limited. On top of this, add the amount spent by state and local governments, and you get to $10.1 Trillion or $1.15 Billion per hour. That means we can fund our federal and state governments for 52 minutes if we tax the entire net worth of an entrepreneur with $1 Billion.

Just think about that again. Jeff Bezos has a net worth of $200 Billion. If we took everything Jeff Bezos owns, including his house, his car, all his shares of Amazon, etc., we could fund the federal and state governments for a little over seven days. So, what Jeff Bezos has accumulated since 1995 by building an online store that sells nearly everything in the world and ships it to your doorstep in less than two days, would all be spent by the state and federal governments in one week. But then what would we do? How many more entrepreneurs would we have to feed to the money-hungry government to keep it running? At some point, the "tax the rich" crowd will need to admit that the solution is not to tax the bright minds of our society who are working to solve important problems and give their money to the wasteful, corrupt government.

The solution is to fix how the money is spent. In the interest of moving society closer to the ideal one we defined throughout the book, a proposal is now suggested to the crowd we cannot agree with. Although we have been against income taxes throughout the book, a compromise seems necessary. Of all the money spent by the government, only about 10%, or $1 Trillion, is for the military. A majority is spent on social programs like Social Security, Medicare, Medicaid, etc. Whether we should cut the military budget is a conversation for another day. In the interest of making this quick and simple, the proposal is to take all the money spent by the government, minus the military, and distribute it evenly amongst the 142 million taxpayers.

Doing so would give every taxpayer $63,000 of supplemental income. This would be even more than a $63,000 salary increase because they would not need to pay taxes on it. It would go directly into the citizens' pockets. Compare that to the 2020 Median Personal Income, according to the U.S. Census Bureau, of $36,000.[15] A person in the 50th percentile would nearly triple his yearly income. In exchange for this, all social programs will end. There will be no more Social Security, healthcare aid, public schools, or anything else. We will completely take the government out of the economy. And immediately, you will see that the $63,000 of supplemental income gets you much more than what the government provided.

Instead of Social Security, you will save your own money. You will invest in the stock market if you want to take some risk or buy corporate bonds for less risk. If that is even too risky, you can purchase government bonds. They are no riskier than Social Security. With both government bonds and Social Security, you don't lose money unless the government chooses not to pay its obligations. For healthcare, you will buy a free market insurance policy and go to a free market hospital if needed. In today's un-free market, insurance costs about $6,000. That number would go down now that the government is out of the picture. In addition, you will put aside $10,000 each year for an emergency, just in case. If you have a child, you will send them to a private school. The average private school costs $16,000. If you don't have a child, you will keep the $16,000 and use it for anything else you want. What about public transportation? You will take a private bus. If the government didn't operate buses, why wouldn't a private company do it? Just like the private companies that operate busses between cities, or to and from the airport.

What does the government provide to you that you cannot buy yourself if the money was given to you instead? For the essential things that the government must provide to protect our rights, like a functioning court system, fire departments, police, and Congress, the costs are a few hundred billion. It is a minuscule amount compared to the trillions we spend. See for yourself here:

https://usgovernmentspending.com/ united_states_total_spending_pie_chart.

The question is: "Are you really getting $63,000 worth of benefits from the government?" If not, then why would you be against this plan?

After the first year of distributing money like this, we hope that everyone will realize that the problem is the truly wasteful government and accept that more taxes on the rich are not needed. They will realize that $63,000 is actually more than enough to cover their basic needs, and they live an even better life now than what the government could have ever provided. In the second year of our policy, we will cut the distribution by about 20%, down to about $49,000, which is still more than enough for anyone to sustain themselves. We must do this because the total revenue we currently bring in is about $8 Trillion. Each year, the government goes further into debt to fund its operations. We can no longer afford this. In the third year, we will begin paying back our debt. If we reduce the distributions to match the Median Personal Income of $36,000, we could afford to pay back $2 Trillion of our debt per year. Keep in mind that $36,000 is a significant amount of money. Half of all Americans live for less than that every year. Of course, now they have to buy directly what the government provided indirectly, but they have double the income to do this and a more efficient market to buy from. Eventually, once the debt is paid off, we can taper off the taxes.

CHAPTER 13

Financial Crises and The Boom-Bust cycle

Alright, so we do not want the government to tax, subsidize, regulate, set prices, bailout corporations, or partake in tasks that can be done by private companies. But we need the government to help us after a financial crisis, right? There is a cycle of prosperity and an eventual collapse in free markets, right? Actually, the boom-bust cycle is mostly due to Central Bank intervention. Without Central Banks, these cycles would be mild and self-correcting. To understand the dynamics, we need to grasp a few concepts first.

Time Value Of Money

If you had an option to receive $100 right now, or $150 in a year, you might choose the latter. If the choice was $100 now or $110 in a year, you might choose to take the $100 now. When comparing $100 now and $(100 + x) in the future, there is some value of "x," for which you would be indifferent about having $100 now or $(100 + x) in a year. In our case, "x" is between 10 and 50, since you found $10 extra not motivating enough to wait a year and $50 extra to be worth the wait. The value of "x" here is an important number. When expressed as "x %," it is your preferred interest rate over a period of time.

The fact that you would forgo $110 in the future for $100 now implies a higher value associated with closer time horizons. Another way to think of it would be to say that future values are discounted by some amount. A $110 gift card in the future is worth less than a $100 gift card right now, even though $110 is bigger than $100. Why is the present more valuable than the future?

Because if you had the money now, you could spend it on goods and services, use it to build a project, or really just do anything. If you receive the money in a year, you cannot do all that you wanted to for an entire year, so there is a cost to waiting. There is also a risk in waiting. For example, you may be hit by a bus during that one-year period. Humans prefer now to later because now is certain, and it is instant. Therefore there must be some benefit that justifies the wait; that is what the interest rate is for.

When there are multiple people involved, there exists an equilibrium interest rate in the market. This market is comprised of those who want to borrow money and those who want to lend money. The interest rate in this market can then be seen as the cost of borrowing money. Just like any other market, the price of borrowing money is determined by market forces. In the interest market, the suppliers are the members of society who have saved some money and want to lend it, and the demanders of money are members of society who want to borrow money for any reason.

We had walked through the consequences of price-setting in markets. The market to borrow money is no exception to this. We will see that the financial crises we experience are entirely due to the Central Bank setting prices in the money borrowing market. It does this by setting the interest rate. Before seeing the consequences of this, we must understand more about the interest rate's role in society.

What Is The Role Of The Interest Rate?

Let us consider a society in an isolated jungle with a population of two people. There are also many animals in the jungle, which the two individuals can hunt.

Today is the first day of the thought experiment, so Hunter 1 and Hunter 2, let's call them Alex and Billy, own nothing. Since they know they will die without food, they begin the hunting process. Without any tools, the only strategy is to spot an animal and chase it until the animal collapses from exhaustion, at which point the hunter captures it. This process takes 8 hours, so each can hunt two animals per day before having to sleep. Alex and Billy each wake up every day and go in different directions to spot animals. They chase them, catch them, bring them home, and eat.

One day Alex thinks of a better way to hunt. He has a visionary idea. He wants to tie a sharp rock to a stick. He calls this invention a spear. If he can build a spear, he will not have to chase the animal for a whole day, but instead, just throw the spear from afar. This way, he predicts he can hunt an animal every 4 hours, thus, doubling his productivity. Alex has just found a way to become more efficient.

He wants to begin his spear-making venture but realizes that building the spear will take him an entire day. If he builds the spear, he will not have food for that day, and he will die. Alex is frustrated. He knows that he could double his productivity if he could just build his spear. However, he cannot because if he takes a day off to build, he will not have food.

He goes to his friend Billy for help. If Billy could cover him for one day, he could build his spear and continue hunting the next day. He asks Billy if he could borrow 1-animal for a day and give him 1-animal the next day. Billy enjoys consuming his huntings in the present, so he is not looking too favorably at this offer. Billy, like all humans, prefers today to tomorrow. He demands that Alex pays his debt with 2-animals the next day to account for Billy's discomfort. Alex accepts, and knowing that he will not starve, he builds his spear for the entire day. He meets Billy at night and enjoys one of Billy's animals.

The next day, Alex hunts 4-animals since he is twice as efficient now. He pays Billy the 1-animal he owes plus the 1-animal borrowing cost. The balance is settled, and from this day on, Alex will output 4-animals daily.

In economic terms, Alex had an idea that could make society more efficient. He was going to **invest** in a project and needed to **borrow**; therefore, he reached out to someone with **savings** to see if they could **lend**. The **interest rate** on this transaction was 100% overnight. Alex produced a useful tool, **capital**, which ultimately made **society** more **efficient.** We know this because, before the venture, society outputted 4-animals total, and now it outputs 6-animals total. Alex benefits because he can now eat more every day, but Billy also benefits because now that Alex brings in more food, he will be more willing to lend some to Billy when Billy wants to fund a venture.

Most people understand the basics here, but one fact is often neglected. Notice that investments were possible because of savings. If Billy had nothing to give, Alex would not have been able to go on his venture and build tools that increased total production. Lesson one is that savings are essential to improve society.

Lesson two comes from noticing what kind of information the interest rate conveys. The interest rate in the example is 100% overnight, so 1-animal today must be paid back with 2-animals tomorrow.

What if Alex had to borrow for two days instead of one? What if, on Day 1, Alex borrowed 1-animal. The next day, he would owe 2-animals to Billy. However, on Day 2, instead of paying the debt, Alex delays his payment to Day 3. How much should he owe? We can view what Alex did as two separate transactions: Days 1 to 2 and 2 to 3 separately. What he borrows on Day 1 gives him a balance due of 2-animals on Day 2. At this point, he begins a new transaction, in which he borrows two extra animals. With these, he pays his debt from Day 1. In essence, he pays his debt with new debt. His old transaction is complete, but his new transaction requires that he pay back the 2-animals he borrowed plus interest on Day 3. Therefore, he owes 4-animals on Day 3. We can also see it as Alex's debt doubling each day. Another name for this is compound interest for those who may be familiar with the term. Alex's debt goes, 2,4,8,16,32... every day.

Alright, so what would happen if Alex's spear project took two days instead of one? Since he needs to eat on both days, Alex must borrow one animal on Day 1, to be paid on Day 3, and another on Day 2, to be also paid on Day 3. When the payment time comes on Day 3, he will owe four animals from Day 1 and 2 animals from Day 2. This means that going on a two-day venture would cost Alex six animals. If his productivity rises to four animals per day once he has the spear, and it takes him two days to build it, the venture would not be possible. Because, on Day 3, Alex will need to pay his debt of six, but he will only have hunted four animals that day.

Technically, Alex can play with his debt to make it a bit easier for him to repay. On Day 3, he can consume one of his animals and use the remaining three to reduce his debt from six to three, but then the next day, the debt will again double to six. So Alex would again have no way out. To simplify the analysis for this example, we can ignore such debt maneuvers by Alex. However, skeptical readers need not worry, as this simplification does not invalidate the analysis. Because, for any given venture, there exists an interest rate that would make the venture impossible.

Some readers may be thinking that the only problem here is that Billy is greedy. If Billy did not ask for a 100% interest rate overnight like an evil capitalist, Alex would have been able to pursue his project. This seems to be the case because we did not yet emphasize something important. During the time of Alex's venture, Billy is living on one animal a day. If this is below the standard diet, there are only a limited number of days Billy can remain alive before the fruits of Alex's venture show up. The time duration of all ventures must therefore be limited.

In a market, independent actors convey this time preference to those who want to venture via the interest rate. Whatever venture Alex goes on, when the time comes, must yield more than what the debt has built up to by then. There is a time limit on ventures because society is living below its means during the venture, but it can only do so for so long. Whatever this time limit is, projects must yield their fruit in this much time or less. This time duration is conveyed using the interest rate.

The persistent readers may still not be satisfied with the fact that we assumed Billy would not be able to sustain himself on one animal a day. Suppose this is not the case. There still must be some lower limit Billy cannot exceed without dying. Maybe it is half an animal, maybe it is less, but the point is that there must be some limit. Then, this limit will determine some maximum time horizon Billy can wait until he needs to receive his interest payments. The idea is challenging at first, especially when multiple people are involved, but it really comes down to something simple. While an individual spends time building tools, he is not spending time covering his basic needs. To not die, he needs to rely on the savings of others during the time length of the project. If the project takes longer than the savings can sustain him, he will be unable to cover his basic needs at some point and will need to abandon the project. The individual planning on building a tool understands how long society is willing to sustain him using their savings via the interest rate.

Alex's two-day venture was not possible in a daily 100% interest rate environment, but the one-day venture was possible. The interest rate told Alex if his venture was possible or not. Only if the interest rate were lower, or if Alex's project resulted in more productivity, or if it had yielded faster, would he have been able to pursue this project. So we can put it this way: *when the interest rate is high, the entrepreneur's venture must have a high [productivity increase] per [project completion time] ratio.* If the interest rate is lower, projects that lead to milder increases in productivity and take longer time can be embarked on.

Manipulation Of The Interest Rate

Let's remember that this thing we call the interest rate is nothing but the price of borrowing money. The determination of the interest rate by a Central Bank is analogous to the government setting prices in any other market. Having analyzed the effects of price setting in previous chapters, we can similarly conclude that interest rate setting is harmful.

Recall that if the price of lumber increases, it is a signal from the market that this certain commodity is under tight supply. If the government sets a price ceiling below market price, it does not magically solve the issue of scarcity. Instead, what happens is a severe shortage. Fewer suppliers want to sell at the lower price, but more buyers want to buy at the lower price. The mismatch also means that only those lucky buyers who happen to find the lumber before it runs out are able to buy it, leaving many other unlucky buyers with zero lumber, even though these unlucky fellows would have been glad to pay more than the ceiling price. There now are unsatisfied buyers who would like to pay more to at least have some lumber rather than none and unsatisfied sellers who would like to sell lumber to these unhappy individuals. Interventions in the market disrupt communication, leading to unsatisfied suppliers and demanders.

So what are the consequences of price setting in the interest rate market? Just like how price setting in the lumber market disrupted the communication between lumber sellers and buyers, price setting in the interest rate market will disrupt the communication between lenders and borrowers. It is critical that lenders and borrowers effectively communicate because of what the interest rate represents:

the length of society's sustenance period with its current savings. When the interest rate is artificially manipulated, the borrowers receive false signals about society's savings.

First, let us consider what happens if the interest rate set by Central Bank policy is higher than the market equilibrium interest rate. Though the Central Bank would probably never attempt this, we can still hypothetically consider it. At the high interest rate, more people would be willing to save, but few investors could go on ventures at such high interest rates. It is beneficial for society to invest its savings because the investments give society better tools, which result in higher productivity. When interest rates are set higher than equilibrium, society has enough savings to sustain itself during ventures, but entrepreneurs are hearing the opposite false signal from the market, which is that there are not sufficient savings, and thus scrap some project ideas.

A good intuition to have for the interest rate is to see it as something that conveys information about time. Precisely, the length of ventures before they bear fruit. So entrepreneurs, in a higher than market interest rate environment, would still go on ventures, but these would be shorter ventures than what could actually be sustained by society. As in, society could withstand the waiting period of a more extended project, but the entrepreneurs only pursue fast yielding ventures. The harm to society is that, although an entrepreneur may have in mind a longer project, which will lead to higher productivity, he can only pursue short-term projects that still increase productivity, but to a lesser extent. All could be summarized as an under-utilization of savings, leading to a slower increase in productivity.

The Central Bank often does the opposite, which is to lower the interest rate below the equilibrium market interest rate. The desire here will be to stimulate the economy. While it is true that the economy will indeed be stimulated, what the Central Bank will not mention is the consequence of this stimulation.

A short-term boost in the economy will follow because of the alteration of the market signals. What society will experience is the opposite of the under-utilization of savings. The low interest rates will falsely signal to entrepreneurs that society has a glut of savings and can sustain itself during the long time horizon ventures. As a result, entrepreneurs will begin their ventures that will not bear fruit until a long time later—longer than society can wait for.

Initially, the effect will be stimulatory because the entrepreneurs will begin ventures, and new businesses will be founded with new jobs are created. However, the booming market will eventually bust because the truth will ultimately come out, which is that society does not actually have enough savings to sustain itself before the completion of these ventures. This will lead to an inevitable bust, where the ventures that were started are terminated before they could bear fruit. This is what we call a financial crisis. The crisis will be blamed on the free market, but the real culprit is the unfree interest rate market, which gave entrepreneurs the false signal that there were enough savings to sustain society until the completion of their projects.

The dynamics are easy to see on a hypothetical island with one individual. For example, if the sole individual on an island ate 1 banana per day and had a saving of 5 bananas, he could only go tool-building for a maximum of five days before realizing he ran out of food. If his eyes are blurry and he sees 10 bananas in his stash, similar to how the Central Bank signals that society has more savings than it actually does, the islander may decide to go on a 10-day venture. However, after 5 days, the truth will catch up to him, and he will need to abandon the project and rush to grab his last banana.

In a populated society, the idea is the same. Different individuals begin different ventures at different times. Some event happens, leading to maybe one entrepreneur abandoning his project, but this does not concern anyone. Later, a few more do. As the entrepreneurs that abandon projects rush to the insufficient savings, more entrepreneurs wake up and catch up to reality. Some day, a panic starts, as people begin to realize that society has not actually saved as much as previously believed. This is modern society's version of a rush to the last banana.

As for the detriments to society, there is the issue of wasting resources. All the projects that began used up resources but never yielded anything. After the crash, perhaps some of those resources may be recovered, but even that will require some amount of work. So the lowering of the interest rate is stimulatory because it leads to the pursuit of more ventures, but this boom is unsustainable and always ends with a bust. We then realize that the boom was actually artificial and that resources should not have been allocated to the ventures to which they were allocated. These failed companies are then scrapped and forgotten about, but the harms are irreversible. Resources are scarce, and everyone in society has an interest in making the most out of the resources. When resources are misallocated with an artificial boom, we are less productive overall. This means we solve cancer later, lift people out of poverty slower, and delay discoveries on lengthening human lives. Everything is tied to productivity, which is tied to our ability to make suitable investments.

The Cure Is More Of The Disease

Unfortunately, the story does not end there. The rush to savings during the crash is sometimes called a liquidity crisis. Liquidity just means money, and money just means our savings. Unlike the island, society does not save bananas; instead, these pieces of paper called U.S. Dollars that entitle you to bananas. A liquidity crash is a rush to money, so just a rush to savings. The issue is that after a crash, the Central Bank, also known as The Federal Reserve in the United States, will decide to help out in the recovery from the crash. Since the crash happened because of a rush to liquidity, the FED thinks it would be a good idea to add some liquidity to the market. It does this in mainly two ways.

First, the FED provides liquidity to the market by buying assets. The FED sees government bonds as the safest asset and therefore buys them. The FED now has government bonds, and the bond sellers now have money. If the bond sellers are people who have bought government bonds before as an investment, they will now have money. If the bond seller is the government, it will eventually have to spend this money in the private sector. Either way, the liquidity crisis will be relieved.

One problem, though. When the FED buys government bonds like this, it reduces the yield on the bonds. Bond yields are similar to interest rates. A purchaser of a bond gives some money to the bond issuer now and receives more money at a later time. Some bonds also have payments to the purchaser called coupons, but without going into details, the basic function of a bond is to borrow money now and pay later. As the yields, so the "interest rates," drop on government bonds, all other bond yields drop, such as the bonds that private companies issue. This is because government bonds are seen to be the safest, and no individual will lend to a private company if it can lend to the U.S. government for a better yield. In general, we should understand that purchasing government bonds lowers the cost of borrowing in the broader market.

The second way to inject liquidity is by directly reducing the interest rates. Again, without too much detail, the FED has an interest rate it pays to banks and also an interest rate at which banks can borrow from the FED. By lowering these rates, the FED incentivizes banks to keep less money with the FED and more in the broad market, thereby increasing liquidity again.

The problem is that, whichever way the FED injects liquidity, the outcome is a reduction in the cost of borrowing. Remember, this was precisely why we had a crash in the first place. Lowering the interest rates below the market rate, meaning reducing the cost of borrowing below what the market deems correct, leads to an artificial boom, which always ends in a bust. The FED's cure to the bust is another artificial boom, which of course, works on the surface, but then leads to an even bigger crash. The FED's cure is more of the disease.

The Ultimate Crash: Who Will Bail Out The Government

Artificially low interest rates lead to an artificial boom, followed by an inevitable crash. The crash is "alleviated" with a further reduction of the interest rates, thereby starting a new artificial boom. By doing so, we worsen the next crisis that is bound to happen because instead of the bust, which would have brought us back to reality, letting us restart by making the proper investments this time, we again choose to lie to ourselves by lowering the interest rates, doubling-down on the policy that led to the crash. Instead of swallowing our bitter-tasting medicine now, we keep choosing to swallow it later, which makes one wonder how this will all end?

In 2020, the government's response to the pandemic caused a minor crash. The FED again reduced interest rates again down to nearly zero and began truly massive amounts of QE. As expected, each QE ends up having to be larger than the previous QE because each bust contains within it the previous busts we never dealt with. Although the consensus is that we seemingly "recovered" from this 2020 crash, the public is in for a surprise. The big catch-up to reality will happen once people realize that the FED cannot play this game forever. And once that happens, the crisis will be bigger than the recession of 2008.

Surely, it is normal for the reader to be cautious against our economic predictions. There are always people making market-crash predictions. And though we are warning the readers of a financial catastrophe, we are not doing so by predicting a specific geopolitical event, like the eruption of a supervolcano, a third World War, or an alien invasion. In other words, we are not predicting a crash due to an outlandish event. Instead, we are explaining the logic behind the boom and how it must lead to a bust because the boom was artificial. Not because we can see the future, but because we understand the logic. In the same way how you would not be a clairvoyant for predicting that a ball thrown in the air would eventually fall down.

Then, let us carry on and explain how the next crisis will unfold. We will have two choices. The artificially lowered rates will reset to normal because the free market is always right. It is reality, and one cannot escape reality. So either we will let interest rates adjust to free market levels by choice, or the free market takes over by force.

If we go with the first option (The Greatest Depression alongside U.S. Government Debt Default), interest rates will rise to their equilibrium levels. This will happen if the FED manually raises rates as high as the market rate. (Or, it ceases to exist, letting the market be free again.) The rate hike will make most existing businesses unprofitable, and they will fail. This is because these businesses were only possible ventures under the artificially low interest rate environment. When the interest rates rise to their equilibrium levels, the cost of borrowing will rise for these businesses, and their business models will no longer be profitable. As these businesses that should have never existed fail, the rush to liquidity will make it tough on all businesses. Even those that were not formed due to the artificial boom. So even these businesses may fail. In addition, having racked up $30 Trillion of debt, the government will not be able to finance its deficit spending anymore at these higher interest rates and will likely default.

There will be millions left jobless and homeless on the street. Millions of adjustable-rate mortgages will be defaulted on. Banks will fail. Foreign countries will experience the same things, as Central Banking is prevalent in almost every country. Under this much distress, society will undoubtedly turn into chaos.

The second option (Very High Inflation) is to let the market override our Central Bank policy. Recall that, at the end of a boom, there is a rush to savings. On the island, it was a banana. In general, these are "consumption goods." They are the goods we need to sustain our lives. We can apply the lessons of this chapter by just changing "savings" with "consumption goods." The investment stage normally begins because we have enough of these "consumption goods" to sustain us through the investment period. We are given this information via the interest rate. We saw that when the interest rate is lowered artificially, a fake economic boom begins with an eventual rush to consumption goods or savings in the inevitable bust. So if we go with the second option, meaning the FED keeps injecting liquidity in order to keep the interest rates low, the market will correct itself via inflation. The rush to "savings" or "consumption goods" can essentially be seen as a surge in demand for these goods. The freshly printed money pouring into the market will be spent mostly on consumption goods. The prices of these goods will begin rising, which will lead to lenders demanding higher interest rates to be compensated for the inflation. The FED aiming to lower this rising interest rate can inject even more liquidity, but this will raise the price of consumption goods, even more, thereby creating a self-feeding cycle.

At this point, the FED can choose to stop and let interest rates rise to get the first option. But if it keeps the cycle going, the prices of consumption goods will eventually rise to extreme levels. This option is also terrible.

There really is no good way out of this mess, and every second we sustain the artificial boom, the inevitable bust worsens. What you should notice is that in either scenario, the U.S. Dollar loses The first option leads to the government defaulting on its debt, which will erode the trust in the U.S. Dollar. The second option is high inflation, which is again a devaluation of the dollar.

A depression like in the first option, or hyperinflation like in the second option, would mean a "Great Reset" of the financial system. Society will go through some major changes either way. Hopefully, we will realize that markets are nothing but communication tools for independent actors worldwide. When the signals are not disturbed, they can be incredible engines of prosperity. However, whenever there is some intervention, the prosperity potential is diminished. The trend has always been to apply more government to our problems, failing to realize that government intervention is the cause of our problems.

Hopefully, after this next crash, we will not blame capitalism and not ask for more government once again. This time, hopefully, we will learn our lesson. It will be tempting to accept offers of massive spending programs imitating the New Deal after the Great Depression of 1929 or creating a world government to bail us out of this crisis, which may also help with future pandemics or climate change. But we know that precisely the high degree of government involvement in our lives caused this mess in the first place. Americans, and those around the world, must keep a clear head through all the chaos and demand a free market instead.

CHAPTER 14

Concluding Remarks

Over time, the American people let the government grow larger. As the government gained more power, its ability to gain even more power increased. And as the rights of the government increased, the rights of Americans decreased. The federal government now gets away with blatant violations of the Constitution and the Bill of Rights because most Americans do not even know their rights. Moreover, they do not even know that this country is uniquely defined to be one with limited government. They do not know their history enough to understand that this country became the most prosperous *because* it had limited government.

Most Americans now just want to grow the government further because they are promised "free things." As we saw, the public always ends up paying for these "free things" in roundabout ways. The "free things" cost more than any alternative in the free market, and the only ones who benefit from the policy end up being the politically connected elite and government bureaucrats. We must stop selling our freedoms for "free" things. Americans must return to the ideals that this country was founded on.

Regardless of our political party, most of us would agree that the government is not representative of us anymore. In this era of polarization, we can still agree on this one thing: The federal government has morphed into an entity that serves the powerful few at the expense of the common people. *This is our uniting factor.*

Some think that we are heading towards fascism, and some think that we are heading towards communism. Fascism is right-wing authoritarianism, and communism is left-wing authoritarianism.

The common element here is *authoritarianism.*

We actually agree with each other, but we just cannot communicate. Social media algorithms, news networks, and politicians all divide us. Lincoln put it perfectly when he said that "A house divided against itself cannot stand." We are the people of this country; we cannot hate each other, or we will fall into a dictatorship. That is certain. Our divide only benefits the establishment.

Let us stop arguing about whether our governments oppress us with their left hand or their right hand and meet at the common ground:

Rejecting Authoritarianism and Embracing Liberty—while we still have the liberty to do so.

* * *

To emphasize the cost of staying silent:

> *"And how we burned in the camps later, thinking: What would things have been like if every Security operative, when he went out at night to make an arrest, had been uncertain whether he would return alive and had to say good-bye to his family? Or if, during periods of mass arrests, as for example in Leningrad, when they arrested a quarter of the entire city, people had not simply sat there in their lairs, paling with terror at every bang of the downstairs door and at every step on the staircase, but had understood they had nothing left to lose and had boldly set up in the downstairs hall an ambush of half a dozen people with axes, hammers, pokers, or whatever else was at hand?... The Organs would very quickly have suffered a shortage of officers and transport and, notwithstanding all of Stalin's thirst, the cursed machine would have ground to a halt! If...if...We didn't love freedom enough. And even more – we had no awareness of the real situation.... We purely and simply deserved everything that happened afterward."*

— ALEKSANDR SOLZHENITSYN,
THE GULAG ARCHIPELAGO 1918–1956

REFERENCES

[1] U.S. Census Bureau, Income Gini Ratio of Families by Race of Householder, All Races [GINIALLRF], retrieved from FRED, Federal Reserve Bank of St. Louis; https://fred.stlouisfed.org/series/GINIALLRF, December 3, 2021.

[4] Historical Debt Outstanding, retrieved from Fiscal Data https://fiscaldata.treasury.gov/datasets/historical-debt-outstanding/, Oct 27, 2021

[5] Perry, Mark J.. "Chart of the day.... or century?" American Enterprise Institute, 17 January 2021, https://www.aei.org/carpe-diem/chart-of-the-day-or-century-5/

[6] Holly, Mike. "How Government Regulations Made Healthcare So Expensive" Mises Institute, 9 May 2017, https://mises.org/wire/how-government-regulations-made-healthcare-so-expensive

[7] OECD(2019), Health at a Glance 2019: OECD Indicators, OECD Publishing, Paris, pp. 151, https://doi.org/10.1787/4dd50c09-en.

OECD, "Main Economic Indicators - complete database", Main Economic Indicators (database), http://dx.doi.org/10.1787/data-00052-en (Accessed on 2 December 2021) Copyright, 2016, OECD. Reprinted with permission.

[8] Dalmia, Shikha. "The Evil-Mongering of the American Medical Association" Reason, 27 August 2009, https://reason.com/2009/08/27/the-evil-mongering-of-the-amer/

[9] Miller, Benjamin, and North, The Economics of Public Issues, 18th ed. (2014), pp. 6, 7.

[10] DiMasi JA, Grabowski HG, Hansen RW. Innovation in the pharmaceutical industry: New estimates of R&D costs. J Health Econ. 2016 May;47:20-33. doi: 10.1016/j.jhealeco.2016.01.012. Epub 2016 Feb 12. PMID: 26928437.

[11] Jaslow, Ryan. "Hospital costs can vary more than $200,000 for same procedure, government report reveals" CBS News, 30 September 2013, https://www.cbsnews.com/news/hospital-costs-can-vary-more-than-200000-for-same-procedure-government-report-reveals/

[12] Chartr. "Mirror, Mirror On The Wall" Chartr, 8 July 2020, https://www.chartr.co/newsletters/2020/7/8/mirror-mirror-on-the-wall

[13] Winters, Mike. "The best- and worst-paying college majors, five years after graduation" CNBC, 12 February 2022, https://www.cnbc.com/2022/02/12/the-best-and-worst-paying-college-majors-five-years-after-graduation.html

[14] Dungan, Adrian. "Individual Income Tax Shares, Tax Year 2016 " Internal Revenue Service, https://www.irs.gov/pub/irs-soi/soi-a-ints-id1901.pdf

[15] U.S. Census Bureau, Real Median Personal Income in the United States [MEPAINUSA672N], retrieved from FRED, Federal Reserve Bank of St. Louis; https://fred.stlouisfed.org/series/MEPAINUSA672N, March 20, 2022.

CONTACT

For all inquiries email: fmc.andthe.usc@gmail.com

Made in the USA
Middletown, DE
07 December 2022

16192106R00120